THE DEVOURING MOTHER

THE DEVOURING MOTHER

The Collective Unconscious in the Time of Corona

SIMON SHERIDAN

Simon Sheridan

CONTENTS

Preface   1

Introduction   3

Chapter 1: The Devouring Mother   18

Chapter 2: The Acquiescent Children   32

Chapter 3: The Rebellious Children   49

Chapter 4: How Dare You   64

Chapter 5: The Archetypal Mask   74

Chapter 6: Conclusion   85

Appendix A: The Land of the Unfree and the Home of the Safe   95

Appendix B: A Theoretical Discussion on Archetypes   110

References   121
Note to the Reader   123
Also by the Author   125

Preface

All human control comes to an end when the individual is caught in a mass movement. Then, the archetypes begin to function, as happens, also, in the lives of individuals when they are confronted with situations that cannot be dealt with in any of the familiar ways.

Carl Jung, Essay on Wotan

In my first book on corona, I stated that my position was that it was a mass hysteria facilitated by the internet. The cornerstone of my analysis was that we invoked what I call The Plague Story even though corona is clearly not in the magnitude of a plague. This raised the question of why that happened and throughout that book I gave a number of different answers some of them cultural, some political and some psychological. But I always had the nagging feeling that I was missing something fundamental. Early in 2021, I began reading the great Swiss psychologist, Carl Jung's, *Red Book* which was personally revelatory on a number of levels. That led me into more of Jung's material and eventually on to the essay on Wotan, which was his explanation for the Nazi phenomenon. Something clicked. It was the above quote which really struck home not least because Jung uses the phrase "mass movement" which is almost the same as my "mass hysteria". It's in a mass movement that the archetypes begin to function according to Jung. For WW1 and the Nazi movement, he identified Wotan as the driving archetype. I had already had the intuition that the corona event was like the wars and I felt strongly that I'd been missing something fundamental. Was that something fundamental an archetype? I asked myself the question: what archetype has been driving the corona event? But, I'd already had the answer floating around in my head even though I didn't know what to do with it: The Devouring Mother. That was like the key which undid the lock. I started to work through The Devouring Mother archetype and everything just fell into place. That is how this book came into being.

This book is short, but not for want of material. Archetypal analysis is almost limitless. Jung was very explicit that the content ascribed to an archetype is not the *essence* of it. An archetype is part form and part energy. It comes together like a constellation and like constellations has a certain inherent subjectivity to it. It is this which most offends the materialist scientific dogma which predominates in the modern West. I have worked within that dogma my entire adult life and I know very well how it functions at a practical level. In the appendix, I will provide my theoretical justification for Jungian analysis and explain why it is a category error to apply materialist science methods to the domain of psychology. The reader looking for an overview of how I understand archetypes may want to read that first although I have sprinkled bits of theory throughout the book and there's no technical jargon in the writing that should inhibit understanding. Reductionist science draws boundaries to enable calculation. Archetypal analysis draws boundaries because otherwise it would go on forever. I think of archetypal analysis as like a spider's web. It branches out in all directions and could eventually encompass the whole world. With this book I have deliberately limited myself to the inner parts of the web, the lines most proximal to the centre: the archetype. In that way, I hope that what the book lacks in quantity it makes up for in quality but I leave the reader to judge whether that is true.

Introduction

The archetypes are the set of psychological patterns, forces or behaviours that we each inherit at birth. They manifest in us in much the same way that language manifests as an automatic process in development. In fact, Jung's theory of the collective unconscious is directly analogous to the Chomskyan notion of Universal Grammar that revolutionised linguistics in the 20th century and aimed to explain how children learn language. Jung believed the archetypes to have an autonomous existence. They were independent of humans but were the impetus for much human behaviour. When Jung asserted that Wotan was driving the events in Nazi Germany, he meant that literally. In less secular ages, one would have said that Hitler was possessed by the devil and that's kind of what Jung meant too. Because our metaphysics does not allow us to say that Hitler was possessed by the devil, we have simply turned Hitler into the devil. In the secular West, if you unironically refer to something as "evil" people will think you're some kind of religious nut. Call the same thing "fascist" or "Nazi" and they won't bat an eyelid. The meaning behind the words is identical but "fascist" has a quasi-secular ring to it. The unfortunate part is that the word "fascist" has a literal, historical meaning and distorting that meaning reduces our understanding of it just at the time when our societies have lurched in that direction. Now more than ever it would be useful to have a very clear understanding of the meaning of "fascist" in its historical sense but that is sadly absent from our language these days. In any case, Jung's way of thinking is at odds with the extremist materialist philosophy that dominates current Western thought. The archetypes are not testable and not amenable to the scientific reductionism that is our default criterion for truthfulness. Of course, corona has revealed the deep flaws that exist in applying scientific reductionism to the living and breathing biological and psychological world that we all live in. What better time to expand our criteria for truth.

I got my first inkling that corona was touching on something deep and dark down in the depths of the psyche from a couple of direct encounters with some people I know. Obviously, there have been all kinds of crazy things to be seen on television and the internet throughout corona, but it was two face-to-face conversations that really struck me as odd early on. They took place at the end of lockdown number one here in Melbourne, Australia. During a conversation with a person I have known for quite a while, the subject of corona came up. I said something that contradicted the dominant narrative. I didn't say it in a confrontational manner or to make any kind of broader point. It was just an offhand comment delivered in a very casual and non-threatening way. Nevertheless, the person I was talking to raised their right arm over their midriff in a protective gesture as if I was about to punch them. What was weird was that they seemingly did not realise they had done it. It was a purely unconscious reaction and something I had never seen from this person or any other person that I can recall in my life. It struck me as deeply weird at the time but I didn't think much more about it.

Then I had a conversation with another person who was, up until 2020, a logical and rational human being; arguably too logical and rational. The subject of corona came up and with this person I was more forthcoming in my views as he was somebody I thought I might be able to have an open conversation with. I was wrong. But what was notable was not that we disagreed but that his argumentation was completely illogical. This is a person who makes his living from logic and who had previously taken great delight in pointing out the logical absurdities of public and political discourse. He's one of those people that thinks if only reason and logic could be applied to public affairs we would all be living happily in utopia. In any other circumstances, he would have been fully aware that he was speaking basic logical fallacies. But not now. As the conversation proceeded, nothing he said made sense and when I pointed out a couple of flaws in his logic he responded with complete non sequiturs. It's one thing to disagree with somebody, it's quite another when their entire argument is illogical and it's another thing again when the illogic comes from somebody whose whole identity was based on being rational and logical. It was like talking to a different person or, rather, like talking to a zombie. In both of these cases, I got a very strong sense that something had "possessed" these two people. I simply wasn't dealing with the same person I had once known. It was only once I started to think more about Jungian psychology that I have taken seriously the idea that these people and millions more like them really have been possessed by something. In and through them, a force has been at work. An archetype has taken over our lives in the same way that an archetype took over at the beginning of WW1 and continued right on through the Nazi regime until the end of WW2. Unlike Jung, I am not familiar enough with mythology to come up with a Wotan equivalent, so I have decided to use one of Jung's own archetypes to explain it: The Devouring Mother.

We all know The Devouring Mother at some level as it is an extension of the natural relationship between mother and child which needs to exist in the early stages of life when the infant is completely reliant on the mother for its existence. In the normal course of development, the child learns to become successively more independent of its mother but along the way there will be times when the mother is too over-protective. Mostly, the child will try to assert independence and the mother will yield it as appropriate. It's when the mother does not yield that things can start to go wrong and if the mother is not yielding due to her own insecurities leading to her not wanting to let go at all, she can become a Devouring Mother. The Devouring Mother archetype occurs when both mother and child are in a dysfunctional relationship of co-dependence in which the mother is just as trapped as the child. The guilt, however, lies with the mother as it is the parent's duty to ensure the child's proper development. Of course, the process of letting go is not easy. Many mothers cry on the first day the child goes to school for this occasion represents the growing independence of the child. Similarly, in tribal societies, when the male child (for it was almost always the male) was taken away for initiation the mother would wail and cry as the boy was now becoming a man and the mother's role in his life was about to be changed forever. It is precisely this independence and autonomy that The Devouring Mother prevents her child from attaining. She wants it to remain perpetually dependent and she does this out of her own insecurity and selfishness. The key reason why The Devouring Mother is relevant to the corona event is because one of the main ways The Devouring Mother attempts to justify her unconscious intentions is on the pretext of *protecting the child*. This protection is necessary when the child is an infant. The problem occurs when protection turns into over-protection and hampers the child's development but that is something that will happen slowly and almost invisibly until one day you've got a 30 year old grown man living in his parents' basement playing computer games all day. In the middle of 2021, the Prime Minister of Australia, whose Treasurer had just delivered a "woman's budget" (perhaps we should call it a "Devouring Mother's budget"), said that his primary mission was to "keep Australians safe". All levels of government were doing the same. HR departments sent emails to employees telling them to be safe. Multi-national corporations sent out email campaigns to their customers hoping they were safe. Even my mobile phone carrier changed the tagline on its name telling their customers to stay safe every time they turned on their mobile phone. This was still going on more than a year into the corona event. At the start of corona, we supposedly didn't know anything about the virus but it was now a simple statistical fact that the sars-cov-2 virus was as dangerous to me as a seasonal flu and it became progressively less dangerous the younger you were. Nevertheless, like all of us, I was being bombarded with the message to stay safe. But that is exactly the excuse that Devouring Mothers use. Is that just a coincidence? Not according to Jung. According to Jung it would be a synchronicity and evidence that an archetype is at work. As we will see, it is one of many such synchronicities that show that it is The Devouring Mother archetype that has been driving corona.

A sceptic might object that it is just common sense that the Prime Minister would want to keep his people safe during a pandemic but this is not true historically. Go back and read the newspaper reports from the 1968 Hong Kong flu, which was the same magnitude pandemic as corona. There was no political response at all. Nobody felt the need to even wear a mask. It's also true that at the start of corona the mission was to "flatten the curve" and to buy time so that the health system would not collapse. That is a very different framing of the situation that has nothing to do with "safety". The Prime Minister of Australia told the nation that everybody would get infected but it was only the elderly and immuno-compromised who were at risk. That was the truth but the message and tone changed almost instantly and "two weeks to flatten the curve" became a distant memory. The thesis of this book is that what happened was that The Devouring Mother took over in the same way that Wotan took over in Germany in the 1930s. The Devouring Mother archetype has been dominant in western society for a couple of decades and the political and social ructions of recent years, most notably Brexit and Trump, represent the first pushback against her ascendancy. With corona, these political ructions reached a new height of intensity. *That* is what was behind the lockdowns and the masks and all the rest which threw out the existing and well established science of public health and led us into the hysteria of 2020 which still has not abated at time or writing (mid-2021). Let's sketch out the dynamic at a high level.

A key feature of The Devouring Mother is that she gaslights her children. This happens in two seemingly contradictory ways. On the one hand, she won't allow any criticism of them at all even when it is necessary and justified. Rather, she suffocates them with false praise. The author D.H. Lawrence, who wrote a lot about the devouring mother phenomenon as he believed his mother to have been a prime example, once wrote in a letter - "I feel I am all the time rescuing my niece and nephew from their mothers, my two sisters; who have jaguars of wrath in their souls, however they purr to their offspring." This *purring* is false praise and false proclamations of love and affection. One of the weirdest examples I ever saw of this at the societal level was a tweet where Corporation X proclaimed that it really loved "you" from the bottom of its heart. Why would a joint stock company, whose only reason for existing is to make a profit for its shareholders, want to proclaim that it "loves" you? You may write this off as marketing bullshit, but it's bullshit that sounds exactly like a Devouring Mother and it's the kind of bullshit that has become more common in recent years. The purring in this case also hides the political realities behind the scenes. Once upon a time, a corporation was put together for the purposes of sailing a ship to collect goods from faraway lands or building a transcontinental railway on a government tender. It achieved its goal and was then disbanded as the shareholders took their profits or losses. Nowadays, corporations hang around interminably where they use their financial power to influence government legislation in their favour. That's not quite Lawrence's *jaguars of wrath* but it does fit the same pattern. It's the hiding of the true intent (greed and will to power) behind a veil of compassion.

While dishing out false praise and empty promises of love on the one hand, The Devouring Mother will be extremely critical, even violent, with her children if ever they should say or do something that threatens the co-dependence relationship that the mother seeks. Her gaslighting has the effect of preventing the child becoming intellectually and emotionally independent, a key part of its overall development. Remember when you were told that if you didn't support the corona measures it meant you wanted old people to die? That kind of emotional manipulation is par for the course with The Devouring Mother. There are a thousand and one ways to keep the elderly safe that don't involve locking healthy people in their house, but those were never discussed. The Victorian Premier, Dan Andrews, showing that The Devouring Mother can take male form, gave what I think might be one of the most succinct expressions of this kind of gaslighting last year. He was asked by a reporter whether he was concerned that his measures, which included curfews and five kilometre travel restrictions, were a violation of human rights. He replied "would you prefer to be on a ventilator?" This was a complete non sequitur. Only the tiniest fraction of the population had any chance of ending up on a ventilator but one hundred percent of the population had had their humans rights removed. The Premier could have answered in a logical, rational way. Instead, he chose to gaslight. Rather than answer a perfectly legitimate question, he gave an answer designed to make the questioner seem dumb, or even heartless, for asking. That's how The Devouring Mother operates. None of the governments in Australia have ever released the "science" they have supposedly been using to justify their measures. In the adult working world, we communicate to each other based on facts and models. A democracy is supposed to involve public debate about the facts and models our elected and unelected officials are using to justify the decisions they make on our behalf. But in the sickly sweet world of The Devouring Mother, we are kept in the dark and given only one option: to acquiesce.

For those who don't acquiesce, The Devouring Mother is also perfectly capable of violence as our police forces have shown. What was particularly interesting about the police response here in Australia was that it was unnecessarily brutal and heavy-handed. The police seemed to be going out of their way to generate resentment from the public. Their behaviour, like the behaviour of my two conversation partners, seemed out of character as if having a source somewhere other than reason. Were they also playing the role of The Devouring Mother lashing out against minor indiscretions out of a sense of insecurity? The most heavy-handed policing has been employed against otherwise law abiding citizens who happened to disobey a corona commandment. One Australian example which went viral was a pregnant woman being handcuffed in front of her children in her own home over a Facebook post. There were countless others. Meanwhile, mass protests such as BLM were seemingly given a free pass. At a time when politicians were calling for unity, they engaged in favouritism. It doesn't make any logical sense but it does make sense within The Devouring Mother archetype. The Devouring Mother is happy to play her children off against each other.

Such emotional manipulations help her maintain the co-dependence relationship.

To my mind, one of the defining features of corona is the complete disregard for the effect of our response on children. This is even more puzzling as it's a simple statistical fact that corona is less dangerous to children than the average flu. This should have been a matter for rejoicing. Instead, in many places children have been kept out of school and, even when allowed to go to school, forced to wear masks and undergo other unnecessary interventions. In Germany and other countries, children were forced to test themselves for corona at the start of the school day while in mid-2021 a video went viral of a ten year old boy explaining what he had to go through at school in the US. What he describes is Devouring Mother behaviour coming from his teachers. This is yet another synchronicity and evidence that the archetype is at work. The Devouring Mother only pretends to be acting to protect her child but with corona there was nothing to protect them from. That would have made a difference if logic was at play. But logic was not at play.

In a similar vein is the mask. The mask is perhaps the ultimate symbol of The Devouring Mother. It purports to keep the wearer safe even though there is no scientific evidence for this claim and plenty of randomised control trials that show masks are useless. Worse than useless, in fact, as we are only now starting to see some evidence of the side effects of long term mask wearing. In any case, you didn't need scientific studies to see that the authorities were making it up as they went. We were initially told that masks were counterproductive and could actually cause more spread of disease as they would be used improperly. Then they became recommended. Then mandatory. Then the recommendation was to wear two. Arbitrary dictates given without rhyme or reason are a feature of The Devouring Mother. What she desires is simple subservience and that's what the mask represents: a very public display of obedience. With mouths covered, the children of The Devouring Mother will not answer back, will not demand their rights, will not ask awkward questions. Silent obedience is what The Devouring Mother wants and, at least symbolically, the mask gives her that. Once again, I must quote the Premier of Victoria who gave us another perfect example of The Devouring Mother at play on the subject of masks. After four months of lockdown and with cases finally back at zero, restrictions had eased in Melbourne. We were heading into summer but masks were still mandatory in enclosed spaces. Some people, perhaps looking to other Australian states where nobody was required to wear a mask, started relaxing their behaviour and wearing their masks below the nose. Andrews tweeted on a Sunday morning something like "Good morning to everybody, except those wearing their masks below the nose." Why was the Premier engaging in unnecessarily divisive behaviour? His tweet was not going to convince a single person to cover their nose. It was inexplicable as a political tactic unless the point was not achieve an outcome but simply to reward the *good children*, to make them feel good and to separate them from the *bad children*. Masks that cover the mouth are a powerful symbol. We will explore their place in the collective unconscious in detail in chapter 5.

The Devouring Mother has been ascendant in the West for several decades. We see her in the metastatic bloat of the modern medical industry. We see her in the relentless gaslighting of the modern media, the ideological drivel that comes out of the universities and our hallucinatory political debate which somehow manages to avoid all contact with reality and all genuine issues of politics. We also see her in a less obvious place, which is the rise of Jordan Peterson from obscure Canadian professor of psychology to worldwide phenomenon. His rise to fame touches on the other half of The Devouring Mother relationship: the children. If Dan Andrews was appealing to the *good children* with his tweet, he was also singling out the *bad children*. In fact, these are the only two pathways available to the child of The Devouring Mother: to rebel or to acquiesce. Jordan Peterson has offered an entire generation raised by The Devouring Mother a way to rebel primarily by the simple act of striving for autonomy and independence. That Peterson would be considered a revolutionary figure speaks to how far The Devouring Mother has become dominant. Most of Peterson's teachings are what would once have been considered plain common sense but in the world

of gaslighting and emotional manipulation where we now find ourselves, common sense threatens the entire order. Whatever one thinks of
Peterson and his ideas, there can be no doubt whatsoever that he tapped
into a deep emotional vein. His book "12 Rules for Life" could just as
well be called "12 Rules for Breaking Free of The Devouring Mother".
Rule 6: clean your bedroom. Do something for yourself. Show some ini-
tiative. In an older time, you cleaned your bedroom or you'd get your
backside smacked. But now cleaning your bedroom becomes a political act. It shows the first inklings of individual will, the development
of autonomy that so terrifies The Devouring Mother. Peterson's infa-
mous interview with Cathy Newman was a direct symbolic confrontation between The Devouring Mother and a strict disciplinarian father.
It had a surreal feel to it. It barely existed on the logical and rational
plane but seemed like a battle between archetypes in the unconscious
itself. Newman spent the entire interview completely misrepresenting
Peterson's arguments; in other words, attempting to gaslight him. A
weaker mind than Peterson's might have lost its grip but Peterson with-
stood the attack. In doing so, he gave a symbolic victory to all those who
have been on the receiving end of the gaslighting of the establishment
in recent decades. That's what made the video archetypal. Peterson had
walked into a trap but he held his nerve and showed that The Devouring Mother was not all powerful after all. In Chapter 2, we will exam-
ine the Peterson phenomenon more closely and see how it relates to the
emergence of what I call *the rebellious children* as a political and cultural
force in the West in the last half a decade.

If Peterson offered a way out to the children who wanted to rebel,
what of the other children; the ones who have acquiesced? Such children have been given false praise while being protected from any and
all criticism about themselves and their work. On the other hand, they
have become exquisitely sensitive to the veiled barbs and emotional war-
fare that goes on in the household of The Devouring Mother. For them,
objective reality is of no concern. They are apt to see a psychological
and political agenda behind every utterance because that is exactly what
has been behind their relationship with their mother (where "mother"

can be both literal and symbolic for the state). When they are eventually forced to confront the real world with all its messiness, it is no surprise that they demand "safe spaces". It's also no surprise that their politics does not seek any actual outcomes but rather is based entirely around establishing the "good people" and the "bad people" where there are no shades of grey but only absolutes, including an absolute assurance in one's own self-righteousness. The children who acquiesce and become part of the co-dependent relationship with the mother can be expected to have not developed into fully autonomous adults. One would expect them to have problems with exercising their will and finding motivation from within rather than without. As it happens, a social media post I saw during corona provides the perfect example of that. It was during Melbourne lockdown number three that happened right in the middle the Australian Open tennis early in 2021. On the Saturday morning on which the lockdown began, a young woman posted how nice it was to wake up during lockdown because it meant she had nothing to do and could happily lie in bed. She went on to thank the Premier. Of course, it takes almost no willpower to organise to do nothing on a Saturday. When the government did it on her behalf, this woman appeared to be genuinely grateful. Some have called this attitude Stockholm Syndrome but it is just another aspect of The Devouring Mother archetype. More specifically, the child who has acquiesced and almost doesn't exist as a separate, adult person separate from the mother. Jung called the confrontation with one's shadow the "apprentice-piece" in the act of individuation (the confrontation with the anima/animus was the "master-piece"). Whether consciously or not, the rebellious children strive for that individuation. That is what Peterson offered them. The acquiescent children do not. They forego the chance at individuation for a false security and there is perhaps no better example of that than lying in bed on a Saturday morning because the government told you stay home. When given in this form it reveals very clearly the psychological aspect of what is going on deep down: the clinging attachment to the "mother" in the form of the state. In Chapter 3, we will explore this psychology in more detail and see that the acquiescent children themselves belong to a Jungian archetype that complements and reinforces the power of The Devouring Mother. It's the relationship between these two archetypes that has been ascendant in the West in recent decades and which drove the corona event.

The phrase Nanny State was coined about fifty years ago in Britain to describe the prevailing form of government which took hold post WW2. Britain, Australia, New Zealand and Canada all share this kind of interventionist government far more than the USA and so it can be no surprise that The Devouring Mother found her most fertile soil in those countries and perhaps nowhere more than here in Australia. We have let The Devouring Mother run rampant. I'm not aware of any other nation which prevented its citizens from leaving the country during corona. In Australia, we had internal state borders closed and even the "borders" around Melbourne shut for four months in one of the longest lockdowns in the world. State Premiers have left residents stranded and unable to return to their houses with snap border closures. Australian citizens languished overseas unable to get home and we even went an extra step and made it illegal for our own citizens to return if they had been in India (a measure that was quickly and quietly re-scinded a couple of weeks after it was implemented, proving at least that there was still a limit on the madness). Once again, none of this had a basis in logic or reason. It is the vindictiveness of The Devouring Mother on display. The *bad children* who left the state or the country apparently didn't deserve our *love*. The same vindictiveness was on display at the state level with individuals unfairly blamed for outbreaks by their own political leaders. Right from the start of corona, our tinpot dictator State Premiers acted like all their Christmases had come at once. In a tweet quickly deleted, Dan Andrews expressed his delight at a photo of an empty freeway that would normally have been full during peak hour. He later felt the need to assure us that he wasn't "enjoying this" as he gave his daily press briefing where, like a good Devouring Mother, he was most anxious to let us know just who was responsible for keeping us safe. He was also not averse to blaming us when things went wrong, including when the wrongdoing was clearly the fault of the government.

The exact same pattern was repeated in Sydney in 2021. Americans have been up in arms about the liberties they have forgone during corona, but they have looked on with horror at what has happened here or in Canada or New Zealand. On this front, the cultural differences between us are very pronounced. Of course, the US once went to war against its "mother" and it celebrates "Independence Day" as a result. One can see why The Devouring Mother would not get as much hold there. Australia and Canada were granted our freedom a little bit at a time and we got free of the "mother country" just in time to come under the even more hegemonic influence of the US empire in the post-war years. As nation states, we are still "young" and clearly not ready or willing to embrace the "freedom" that Americans so prize. I explore this theme in more depth, with a focus on how corona has played out in Australia, in the Appendix.

It is a final and telling synchronicity that with corona we were all locked in our houses. The household has always been the domain of the mother. As a boy, I briefly shared a house with my mother, grandmother and great-grandmother as well as their respective husbands. It was the women who ruled the house. Woe betide the man who dared step foot in the kitchen. The men were usually elsewhere, at work or at the club. If they were home, they were in the shed. The development of the individual takes place as the child successively removes itself from the household, firstly with schooling, then a social life and finally as they move out and become an autonomous adult. With corona we were all returned back to the household, back to childhood, back to our mothers. Defenceless as we were supposed to be against the virus, we once again needed the care and protection of our surrogate mother: the State. "I'm sick of being treated like a child" is a refrain heard many times in 2020-2021, but it seemed to be an opinion that was in the minority. It was in the minority because society had been overcome by an archetype and the archetype demanded that you be a child whether you liked it or not.

What does all this portend for the future? The strange thing about The Devouring Mother is how powerless she really is. All her gaslighting is just sound and fury, signifying nothing. If it were to end tomorrow, we would remember it as nothing more than a delirious fever dream. Her power depends entirely on the willingness of the child to put up with it. Once the child is big enough to decide to go its own way, there is nothing much the mother can do about it. At time of writing (mid-2021), in Western societies the actions of The Devouring Mother are on full and open display. But, almost by definition, that implies the strain in the relationship. When things are good, The Devouring Mother relies on false flattery and feigned niceness. Right now, we are in full on vindictive mode. 24/7 media gaslighting, censorship of even the most tame dissenting opinion and de-platforming are now daily occurrences. There is an element of desperation in the whole thing and there should be because the pathway we have taken has no endpoint. That is not a problem for The Devouring Mother. She does not want an endpoint. She wants the co-dependence to continue indefinitely. That's why the case of Australia is so fascinating because our Devouring Mother did her job and kept us safe. But this left us no way out of the house. We are, at time of writing, permanently grounded, although, sensing that the public had finally had enough, our Prime Minister in early July 2021 finally came up with a plan by which the State will allow us our freedom back. Will such plans work? Maybe. It depends on the *children*. In Florida, Texas and other US states, they already have their freedom back. This shows that the corona event will be over when the public demand its independence. That can happen at any time. But this raises the larger question of where The Devouring Mother goes from here. If she has been ascendant in the last decades and if corona represents a brief takeover, does she relinquish the newfound power or try to hold onto it? If she does relinquish it, do we go back to where we were or does she lose hold altogether? Again, this is not really going to be determined by the mother. We know what she wants: never ending co-dependence. The question is what do the children want. Will corona be the last straw? Will they now demand their independence or will they acquiesce. We will speculate on such questions in the final chapter of the book and see what the archetype predicts for the future.

Chapter 1: The Devouring Mother

Each Jungian archetype has a shadow side to go with its positive attributes. The Devouring Mother is a shadow form of The Mother archetype, although it will be useful for our purposes to use the more generic label of The Caregiver in order to highlight that the psychological pattern can be present at any time in life and in both men and women, although it is mostly a female pattern. Like all archetypes, The Caregiver has its virtues which are generosity, compassion and selflessness. As the name suggests, The Caregiver desires to help others. Nobody needs help and attention more than a young child, hence The Caregiver's stereotypical role in child rearing, but The Caregiver will also do well in other domains where people genuinely need help such as social work, the medical industry or aged care. It is no coincidence that the corona event has been run primarily through the health bureaucracy and the medical industry. That is where we would expect to find The Caregiver. It is also where would expect to find The Devouring Mother because that is the shadow side of the archetype. An old fashioned way to think about this is having an angel sitting on one shoulder arguing with a devil sitting on the other shoulder. Each archetype has its own specific angel and its own specific devil, the virtues it strives for and the temptations it must overcome. The temptations of The Caregiver, which are the attributes of The Devouring Mother, are martyrdom, emotional manipulation and guilt tripping used to control others, enabling behaviours such as encouraging drug addiction and smothering the growth of others. It's worth reviewing an extended quote from Jung here to see his description of The Devouring Mother:

> *First she gives birth to the children, and from then on she clings to them, for without them she has no existence whatsoever. Like Demeter, she compels the gods by her stubborn persistence to grant her the right of possession over her daughter. Her Eros develops exclusively as a maternal relationship while remaining unconscious as a personal one. An unconscious Eros always expresses itself as will to power. Women of this type, though continually "living for others," are, as a matter of fact, unable to make any real sacrifice. Driven by ruthless will to power and a fanatical insistence on their own maternal rights, they often succeed in annihilating not only their own personality but also the personal lives of their children.*

We'll expand on some of these attributes throughout the book but in this chapter our focus will be on the aspect of The Devouring Mother that is most relevant to the corona event, a specific manifestation of the psychology that is well known in our culture by the name Munchausen by Proxy.

Munchausen by Proxy comes out of modern clinical psychiatry and refers to the scenario where a mother either seeks unnecessary medical treatment for her children or actively harms the children in order to get treatment. The mother is responsible in 95% of cases of Munchausen by Proxy and therefore the syndrome fits within The Devouring Mother archetype. Because Munchausen by Proxy is often used in a court of law to either prosecute or defend a mother for the harm of the child, questions of intention arise because lawyers need to establish motive in order to win cases. However, in our archetypal analysis, motive is not necessary. An archetype is a possibility that can manifest at any time just like water can manifest as ice or steam given the right conditions.

Jung emphasised the notion of transformation in his psychology. He believed it was our mission as humans to incorporate the archetypes into the self and ensure we are not overwhelmed by them but, of course, we don't always succeed. For this reason, we can expect varying levels of self-awareness on the part of people manifesting an archetype. Some may be fighting a psychic battle, others may be completely unaware that they have been overwhelmed. Munchausen by Proxy is problematic in a legal context precisely because it does not establish motive and so even the legal system recognises the loss of autonomy that can happen in relation to archetypes.

The rapper, Eminem, was one of the most famous victims of Munchausen by Proxy. His mother would take him to hospital when he was young even though he was not sick. He once wrote a song on the subject which contains the lyric:

"My whole life I was made to believe I was sick when I wasn't/'til I grew up and blew up..."

If ever there was a catchphrase for the rebellious child breaking free of The Devouring Mother it would be that. All you've gotta do is grow up. The Devouring Mother aims to inhibit her child from growing up and Munchausen by Proxy is one way to achieve that goal by gaslighting the child into thinking it is sick. In more extreme cases, the mother goes a step further and actively harms the child. Damage to the child comes in the physical form but perhaps more importantly in the psychological form of deep confusion and anxiety. Consider a simple case of cold or flu. As children, we came down with a fever and started to feel sick but our parents were there to re-assure us that it was "just a cold". They would put us to bed with a lemon drink and tells us everything was going to be okay. Eventually, the fever would break and life would go on as normal. This seemingly banal occurrence hides a deeper wisdom that the corona event has thrown into great relief. Whether they knew it or not, our parents were teaching us to trust our bodies; our immune systems. The recognition was that the flu was just a part of life. There is no *solution* to a flu. It is not a problem to be solved by medical intervention, it is a predicament to be worked through (to use an incredibly useful distinction from John Michael Greer). Our parents had taught us how to recognise a cold or flu and how to deal with it. Once we have learned that, we no longer worry when a cold or flu comes along. As adults, we recognise the symptoms and simply go to bed when fever strikes and let nature take its course. Imagine your childhood if your parents didn't do that but insisted on rushing you to hospital every time a fever struck. Imagine if they went one step further and would rush you hospital when you didn't even have a fever. That would set you up for a life of anxiety around respiratory viral disease and, of course, this is exactly what has happened during corona. People with flu symptoms were told they didn't have the flu, they had *covid* and were then treated like a biohazard. Anybody with a runny nose and a cough rushed to hospitals and testing centres to get tested. Many people with no symptoms whatsoever were given tests that came back positive. Rather than tell them they were fine and everything was going to be okay, The Devouring Mother told them they were carriers of deadly new disease; a disease whose symptoms were, in the vast majority of cases, indistinguishable from the common cold we all learned to cope with as children. In this way the corona event has been an extreme form of gaslighting; the undermining of the simple truths we all learned while growing up; the sowing of distrust in our own perceptions to be replaced with the knowledge of "the experts" using fancy medical tests. No longer can we trust our immune systems. We must blindly trust the experts. In doing so, we become dependent on The Devouring Mother in her Munchausen by Proxy form.

One of the best portrayals of the confusion and disorientation caused by The Devouring Mother that I have seen in popular culture is from the excellent Danish-Swedish television series *Bron-Broen,* known in English as *The Bridge.* In the story, Saga Norén is the lead detective for Malmö police in Sweden and throughout the various series of the show she is paired up with another detective from across the strait in Copenhagen. Norén is the cool, calm and rational Swede playing off against her more emotional and intuitive Danish counterpart. The difference is meant symbolically to reflect the differences between Danish and Swedish culture but, even by Swedish standards, Norén is unusual as she has Asperger's Syndrome and is detached, unemotional and rational to a fault. This makes her very good at her job as detective but no so good at forming close personal relationships. In series three of the show, we meet Norén's mother and find out she is a Devouring Mother who practiced Munchausen by Proxy on Norén's sister when she was a child. Norén is plagued by guilt at her inability to save her sister who later committed suicide. Thus, in The Bridge we get to see the interaction of a gaslighting Devouring Mother against possibly the one psychological type that you would expect to be most immune to that gaslighting; a vehemently independent and accomplished adult with Asperger's Syndrome. However, even Norén struggles to maintain her sanity and keep her rationality intact in the face of her mother who is an expert at manipulation. In this way, the story is true to real life where, in cases of Munchausen by Proxy, the child must be removed from the mother and must stay removed as it is very common for the syndrome to reappear when the two are reunited. The confrontation between Norén and her mother is characterised by confusion. Norén cannot believe what her mother says even though she wants to. She might want to trust her (who wouldn't want to trust their mother) but she knows she can't. This confusion has been evident in the public health measures throughout corona which changed constantly and often directly contradicted what was accepted truth just months earlier. It has now become a running joke that you just have to wait six months for a "conspiracy theory" to become the reality. This comes down to an issue of trust too, a trust in government that, especially in the USA, has been lacking for a long time. Trust comes from stability and from a concord between words and action. If you go to visit a doctor and they keep changing their diagnosis and the kinds of treatment they are giving you for a specific condition, you would probably start to wonder whether the doctor really knows what they are doing. Nevertheless, our public health bureaucrats and politicians did exactly that during corona culminating in perhaps the ultimate form of nonsense when Fauci in the US began recommending people wear two masks. This was less than a year after he was on record saying masks were counterproductive. That is, to be as polite as possible, confusing. Many people found reasons to explain it away. Some people even said it was an example of "science" to change your mind about things. But the fact that they felt the need to make up such explanations already shows that there was cognitive dissonance going on. That's how it is when dealing with The Devouring Mother. The acquiescent child will find reasons to continue to believe in the mother. They will make excuses on her behalf. The rebellious child will not.

To reiterate, Munchausen Syndrome by Proxy occurs when the mother either makes up a story about an illness that never happened or actively harms the child in order for it to appear as if the child is sick. Let's take each of these in turn and see how it applies to corona.

On the subject of made up illness, corona is perhaps a world historical prime example. Whether you believe "covid" is actually a new disease (I still don't understand why it is considered new when it seems to have no unique symptoms), it's a statistical fact that in a great number of "cases", the person shows no symptoms or only mild flu symptoms. This is because we have been mis-using the PCR technology to identify a "case". Is it possible to have "covid", supposedly a deadly new disease, if you have no symptoms? According to our public health bureaucrats, it is. Return a positive test and you will be labelled diseased by the state and you will not only have to endure the stress of wondering whether you will become sick, you will have several weeks of having your life turned upside down while the government tests all your family and friends and while you deal with all the attendant issues on your interpersonal relationships, work and finances. Meanwhile, you are most likely have no symptoms or only mild flu symptoms. Throughout corona, we have been telling people they have a deadly disease even though most barely have any symptoms. The media amplified the signal by talking endlessly about "cases" and never about illness. That is Munchausen by Proxy at the societal level. At best, it is deeply confusing and at worst a form of gaslighting designed to create unnecessary anxiety.

In the more extreme forms of Munchausen by Proxy, the mother will actively harm the child and there is plenty of evidence for this during the corona event, especially in the early days where, for whatever reason, the sedation-intubation protocol was circulated among medical professionals and recommended as the go-to option for treatment of *covid*. It wasn't until a couple of months later that videos emerged of doctors claiming that the disease they were seeing was not the one they had heard about and that the intubation treatment was not the correct protocol. By then, the damage had been done. A harrowing video of a whistle-blower nurse from a New York City hospital showed that anybody suspected of having corona, even those who tested negative, were put under heavy sedation and intubated[1]. The survival rate from such an invasive procedure was extremely low. Around the same time, we started hearing about hydroxychloroquine which got caught up in the madness of US politics after Trump stated that he was using it as a preventative measure. The jury appears to be still out on whether hydroxychloroquine really is effective. Some doctors say it is. Some doctors believe that it also caused unnecessary illness and even death as it was being given in very high doses that compromised the immune system of already vulnerable people and made them less able to fight off the virus. It will probably take years or even decades for the truth to be known, if ever.

These are examples of direct harm from the medical treatment given to patients. How many of the deaths and serious disease attributed to corona were due to these kinds of treatments is a question we will never know the answer to. Nevertheless, there can be no doubt that people were both injured and even died directly from treatments like invasive intubation. There were also certainly deaths caused indirectly by lack of proper care given to those in danger. In all western countries, most of the deaths from corona have come from nursing home patients. Conditions in nursing homes went to hell even before the lockdowns as employees either didn't show up to work or, if they did, gave greatly reduced attention to the most needy. In a number of countries the army had to get sent in to ensure standards of care. Again, we will never know how many of the deaths were due to actual illness and how many were due to treatments and lack of care. On one end of the spectrum are people such as Denis Rancourt who believes almost all the deaths were caused by our response[2]. There are more moderate positions such as the Swiss Policy Research who have done a great job of providing objective data and analysis right from the start of corona. They estimate about 30% of the excess death was caused by the response[3]. To that, we can add the even harder to determine side effects caused by the lockdowns such as suicide, depression, increased drug and alcohol abuse and the economic ramifications which will lead to less money being available for health expenditure in the future. In any case, the response itself caused unnecessary pain and suffering and thereby fits the pattern of Munchausen by Proxy.

It is on the question of the vaccine, however, that the Devouring Mother in her Munchausen by Proxy form shows herself mostly clearly. One could forgive medical practitioners in the early days of corona for over-reacting given the stress of the situation. Doctors are only human and when everybody around you is losing their mind it is no doubt hard to keep yours especially when you are at the coalface. With the vaccine we have no such excuse. At time of writing, we are almost a year and a half into this business and, despite continuing hysterics around every new "variant" that some public health bureaucrat reads into the tea leaves of the viral genome, we know what this virus is. The fundamentals have barely changed from day one. The case fatality rate is about 0.15% with the risk being almost exclusively confined to the elderly and immuno-compromised. For the majority of the population, this virus is equivalent to seasonal flu and, the younger you are, the less dangerous it is. The idea of mass vaccination with an experimental vaccine for such a virus is ludicrous and completely irrational but it is irrational in exactly the way predicted by Munchausen by Proxy where The Devouring Mother insists on unnecessary medical treatments even if she must harm the child to do so. In one of his interviews, Professor Sucharit Bhakdi, who has been one the most lucid experts right from the start of corona, was talking specifically about the dangers of the vaccines and noted "the immune system is being trained [with the vaccine] to do something that it would do very well on its own." With just a couple of changed words, this sentence could describe The Devouring Mother archetype in its entirety. Children grow up and seek independence all by themselves. The parents' job is to keep the children on the rails, not to micromanage every part of their development. But that is what The Devouring Mother does because she wants the child to remain co-dependent. That is what our society does too. Think about all these über safe playgrounds designed so children can't hurt themselves. For previous generations, dealing with a broken bone was just a normal part of growing up. Just like catching the flu, it was an opportunity to learn about the healing powers of your body. Nowadays, that is not allowed to happen. We inhibit the development of autonomy in the young in other ways too. Think of the enormous student debt we burden them with. Think of the fact that in Australia and many other western countries, the dream of home ownership is fast disappearing as rampant inflation makes housing unaffordable. Think that during corona we have added trillions to the national debt which must, at least in theory, be paid off by the young. For a society that claims to care about the young, we sure do a good job of inhibiting their growth and autonomy. All these things make the young less independent and the vaccine follows the same pattern. Rather than allow young people for whom the virus poses no risk to be exposed naturally and let their immune system do a job it's been doing for millions of years, we have locked them away in their houses waiting to "train" their immune system with the vaccine. That would be bad enough except we have no idea what the cost-benefit analysis of the vaccine is. Vaccines such as the tetanus shot have a clear cost-benefit profile. Tetanus is a genuinely deadly disease which will kill everybody who gets it if they do not receive immediate treatment. The side effects of the tetanus vaccine are mild and very well-known as it has been in use for decades. It's a no-brainer to take a tetanus shot. With the corona vaccines, the cost-benefit analysis is not clear at all. Unlike the tetanus shot, the amount of protection the corona vaccine offers is also unknown but we already know it doesn't prevent infection and doesn't guarantee protection from death. An argument could be made that the vaccines are in the interests of the elderly who are most at risk from corona and have

THE DEVOURING MOTHER - 27

nothing to fear from long term effects. In a sane society, we would let the elderly take the vaccine and let everyone else get on with their lives. But we are in the society of The Devouring Mother. In Europe, the vaccines are now being trialled on children as young as six months old. At time of writing, we are hearing the latest fear campaign that corona *could* become a dangerous disease for children and therefore they should take the vaccine too. This is the exact excuse given in Munchausen by Proxy cases where the mother is worried about what *could* happen to her child and demands treatment for things that haven't even happened yet. Of course, anything *could* happen. But it's a simple statistical fact at present that corona is far less dangerous to children than seasonal flu so why would anybody want to vaccinate children with an experimental vaccine? As Bhadki states bluntly – "You are endangering your own children." But that is exactly what The Devouring Mother does in her Munchausen by Proxy form. She deliberately submits them to unnecessary medical intervention, not in their interests, but in hers.

Such unnecessary intervention has become a feature of the medical industry in recent decades. One of the ways in which it has manifested is a seemingly counterintuitive form which involves disintermediating medical professionals. We have seen this exact pattern during corona where the "diagnosis" was based entirely on the PCR test. Normally, if you are sick, you go to a doctor who makes a diagnosis based on your symptoms. That is a skilled activity where the training and experience of the doctor play a crucial role. Of course, doctors don't always get it right. The human body is an extremely complex system and there are many variables at play. The tests that get used in the medical industry are there to help the doctor with diagnosis. They are like the doctor's toolkit and just like any tool they must be used wisely and their results interpreted properly. To give an example from my personal experience. I went to a dermatologist with a skin condition. She made a diagnosis but also took a sample and sent it off for testing. The result came back negative and this contradicted her diagnosis. She was very sure of her diagnosis and reasoned that there was an error in the test. I went in to get another sample taken and this time the test came back positive. We proceeded with treatment based on her diagnosis and the problem went away. That's how it normally works. The test is there to aid the diagnosis, not replace it. It is one bit of evidence the doctor must weigh up among many. What has been happening in the medical industry in recent decades is an attempt to replace a doctor's diagnosis with diagnosis by technology and that is exactly what we have seen during the corona event. Doctors were replaced by the PCR test. To become a confirmed covid "case" did not require a doctor to diagnose symptoms, it just required a test to give a result. Having removed doctors from the diagnosis side of the equation, we proceeded to remove them from the treatment side too. Treatments that came from doctors based on real world experience such as hydroxychloroquine and ivermectin were deliberately suppressed. The only acceptable treatment was the vaccine. It's an irony of corona that many people will tell you that if you're not a doctor then you should keep your mouth shut and leave it to the experts. They don't realise that the doctors themselves have been silenced. In Australia, both doctors and nurses were threatened with de-certification if they spoke out against the vaccines. We saw the same thing in many other countries. The Devouring Mother in her Munchausen by Proxy form will often shop around for a doctor who is willing to give treatment. The treatment is the end in itself. We have seen the exact same thing with corona. The vaccine must be given even though the vast majority of people experience the virus as nothing more than a regular flu and even though the results of the vaccine are unknown.

This pattern of replacing diagnosis by a real human doctor with an automated test has been going on for a few decades. A prime example is the mammogram. Once upon a time, all women were encouraged to get yearly mammograms. You didn't need your doctor to diagnose you first, you just went in and got the test. Sounds like a good idea. Detecting cancer early should give treatment a better chance of working. However, mammograms, like all biological tests, have a false positive problem and because the illness in question is cancer the ramifications of false positives are extreme because cancer treatments are highly damaging to the body. If a false positive leads you to get treatment when you didn't need it, you just went through a lot of unnecessary suffering. It's only in recent years that the costs of the mammogram testing program have been coming to light and there are now a number of experts who claim that such screening programs do more harm than good. Here is a quote from an article titled "Routine mammograms do not save lives":-

> *There are significant harms associated with mammography screening and no reliable evidence of benefit. It is time to discontinue routine mammograms for all healthy women of a particular age. Resources should be shifted toward surveillance of women at higher risk for breast cancer, diagnostic workup for women with a change in their breast that does not go away and for ensuring that women receive timely treatment for a confirmed invasive breast cancer.*
>
> *Population-based mammography screening has opportunity costs for the health care system, not to mention the social, financial, interpersonal and emotional costs to women and their families.[4]*

Substitute the phrase "mammography screening" with "PCR testing" and change the breast cancer references to flu-like symptoms and the above paragraphs serve equally well as a critique of the approach taken during the corona event. The same pattern has played out with other diseases such as thyroid cancer. Automation leads to false positives which lead to damaging treatment. The Devouring Mother in her Munchausen by Proxy form submits her children to unnecessary medical intervention. The replacement of observation and experience provided by a doctor with an automated test controlled by the state manifests the archetype perfectly. The whole corona event was facilitated by the PCR test and on the basis of that test, which even the man who invented the technology (Kary Mullis) said should never be used as a test for viral disease, The Devouring Mother embarked on the unnecessary intervention of overturning society for a virus with a 0.15% case fatality rate that is of no risk to the young and for most people is no worse than seasonal flu. The justifications given were themselves a form of emotional blackmail. We were told that if we didn't want to overturn society and be locked in our houses that we must want old people to die. A leaked German government document early in 2020 stated that most people could see the virus for what it was and the propaganda machine needed to focus on guilt-tripping messages like killing your grandma to win compliance. The document said authorities should focus on presenting images of suffocation as that is a primal fear. About a year later, the Australian government would release an advertisement featuring a woman (an actor) suffocating in a hospital bed. Were the German and Australian governments sharing propaganda techniques or was it The Devouring Mother at work? Later we would start hearing that the virus *could* become a dangerous disease in children just like we had heard initially that the virus *could* kill tens of millions. But this is all just Munchausen by Proxy. The Devouring Mother rushes her child to hospital on the basis of what *could* happen. The Devouring Mother seeks a never-ending relationship of co-dependence and, with Munchausen by Proxy, the co-dependence is maintained through illusory medical conditions or through direct physical harm. The stage is set for exactly these possibilities right now. We have the endless "variants" of covid ready to roll. The elderly will no longer die of pneumonia. They will die of covid or rhivid or whatever other *new* disease can be tested for. All it will take is a virologist to find a *new* virus and create a PCR test and the whole play can start over again.

What is at stake with the removal of trained medical professionals and their replacement with automation is, to come back to Jung's description of The Devouring Mother, *unrestrained will to power*. This will to power came out in a number of ways during corona. One of them was in the guise of heroism. We heard that it wasn't enough to flatten the curve, we must smash the curve. Apparently intelligent people were heard to say that every single person in the world must be vaccinated. We must exterminate the virus. These all sound nice in theory. The question is always at what cost. But cost went out the window very early on. It became impolite to even mention the economic damage that was being done. Governments who had spent decades building a reputation as prudent fiscal managers were suddenly announcing seemingly infinite spending programs and budget deficits all while overturning the assumptions of society over a virus with a 0.15% case fatality rate. That is unrestrained will to power. It is delusional and completely lacking in pragmatism. It also ties in with the other thing that has been impolite to talk about – who is making all the money? Somebody is making money from the tests and the vaccines. Enormous amounts of money. The pattern of automation and reducing the involvement of trained medical professionals matches the stated objectives of powerful interests who want medical care to be completely automated and doctors to be replaced with artificial intelligence. Such programs are not going to win the support of doctors for the most part and so have been run out of the public health bureaucracies where cost savings and other justifications can be given. All this is just will to power; the frankly megalomaniac desire to control the health outcomes of every person in the world alongside the more mundane fact that enormous sums of money are being made in the pursuit of what is a Quixotic delusion, all in the name of "protecting" people. It is all just The Devouring Mother at work.

In cases of Munchausen by Proxy, the child must be removed from the mother. In The Bridge, that is what Saga Norén attempted to do but failed. In real life, however, Eminem succeeded. Not only did he free himself, he was later granted custody of his brother in order to protect him from their mother. Maybe in that story there is a hint as to the direction we need to take in the years ahead.

Chapter 2: The
Acquiescent Children

There are two types of child of The Devouring Mother: the rebellious and the acquiescent. The rebellious children must either break the relationship off altogether and leave the house or otherwise eke out a realm of autonomy. Until either of these is done, the relationship between The Devouring Mother and her rebellious children is going to be unstable. The mother seeks co-dependence and she does that by stunting the growth of the child. Because the rebellious child demands its autonomy, the two are incompatible. The same is not true of the mother's relationship with her acquiescent children. That relationship is an equilibrium position for both mother and child and can continue indefinitely if external circumstances do not intervene. That is the whole problem because the relationship is not a healthy one. The Devouring Mother and her acquiescent child are both in their shadow. Imagine if Luke Skywalker quit The Rebel Alliance (there's that word again) and joined his father working for the empire. That wouldn't be good for him or Darth Vader, who would have lost his chance at redemption. The same goes for The Devouring Mother and the acquiescent child. For Jung, the child archetype in general was symbolic of the individuation process because a child represents the potential to individuate. However, The Devouring Mother deliberately prevents her children from individuating. It is this that the rebellious children are fighting against and this makes sense archetypally. They are striving to become adults which means they are striving to individuate themselves, to come to fruition, to grow and expand and ideally to flourish. The acquiescent child is different. It submits to the mother and accepts being stifled. In so doing it does not come to fruition, does not flourish and gets stuck in a rut. The rebellious children of The Devouring Mother come from all archetypes. All they demand is the freedom to become themselves and to escape the stifling atmosphere of The Devouring Mother's household. There is, however, one archetype which is susceptible to the co-dependence relationship that The Devouring Mother seeks. Up until now I have been referring to this by the phrase acquiescent children but now we can be more specific about it. The archetype in question is The Orphan.

The Orphan bears the characteristics one might expect from somebody separated from their parents as a child. The primary goal of The Orphan is to regain the safety they lost in childhood. There is an implied wound in the nature of The Orphan that comes from the lack of development suffered because of the (symbolic) early separation from its parents. The Devouring Mother tries to continue the nurturing relationship between mother and child beyond the time when it is needed. The Orphan was removed from that nurturing relationship prematurely and suffered developmentally as a result. This is why the two fit together so neatly but the fit is not a positive one. The Orphan's archetypal mission is to heal that wound and make up for the lost development they suffered but they must take ownership of that process. That is their pathway to individuation. The positive traits of The Orphan are realism, empathy and the ability to connect with others. Its shadow traits are playing the victim, excessive complaining, feelings of hopelessness often leading to apocalyptic fantasies and expecting favourable treatment as compensation for its suffering. These shadow traits fit in perfectly with The Devouring Mother. The Orphan can become addicted to being powerless because when one is powerless one gets rescued and made to feel safe. The Orphan's archetypal task is precisely not to get rescued but to learn to do it themselves but that is difficult. Far easier to let somebody else take charge and that is where The Devouring Mother comes onto the scene. A powerless child is exactly what The Devouring Mother needs for her desired co-dependence relationship. The trouble for The Orphan is that lapsing into powerlessness is its shadow side. Its other shadow traits such as playing the victim, expecting favourable treatment and engaging in predatory behaviour towards others also fit in nicely with The Devouring Mother who will happily encourage all of these behaviours knowing (unconsciously) that these are shadow traits that will prevent the child reaching autonomy while also being a weapon against the rebellious children. This is what is known as *enabling* where The Devouring Mother encourages behaviour that is damaging to the child. Sometimes this enabling can be as relatively harmless as encouraging a child towards a goal it cannot achieve and thereby setting it up for disappointment. It can also include more damaging examples such as encouraging a child into drug addiction or crime, two options that relate back to the Munchausen by Proxy pattern we examined in the last chapter.

The best example I have seen in popular culture which captures The Orphan's relationship with The Devouring Mother is the excellent Australian movie "Animal Kingdom". The protagonist of the story, J, is both an archetypal and a literal Orphan. In the first scene of the movie, we learn his mother has just died from an overdose. We don't know where his father is, but he's obviously not around as J must call his estranged maternal grandmother, Smurf, for help. We find out that J's mother had deliberately kept him away from Smurf and as the movie unfolds we learn why. Smurf, played by Jacki Weaver, is the matriarch of a crime family. Weaver's performance is certainly one of the best examples of The Devouring Mother in film, all the more so because her character is completely unaware of her actions. Her enabling behaviour is to induct a young man who is almost legally an adult but developmentally still a child into a life of crime. In this way, the movie is a paradigm example of the destructive relationship between The Devouring Mother and The Orphan. As the viewers, we know full well that J must escape from the relationship and the film provides two ways out for him in the form of a well-meaning police officer and a romantic relationship. Both offer The Orphan a way to fulfil his archetypal need to build a life for himself and escape the clutches of The Devouring Mother. I don't think it will spoil the film's ending to say that J finds his own way to escape in a brilliant twist which is archetypally both a victory and a defeat. He fulfils The Orphan's need to take responsibility and control and breaks free of The Devouring Mother. The final scene captures the archetypal meaning of this brilliantly as The Orphan transcends the relationship but only by going to the dark side in another way. J escapes. Other Orphans do not. The writer D.H. Lawrence spoke of having to rescue his nieces and nephews from their devouring mothers and, while such relationships are rarely as toxic as that depicted in Animal Kingdom, this is what must happen especially in the case of The Orphan which is the archetype most likely to get trapped by The Devouring Mother.

The Orphan is the necessary other half of The Devouring Mother archetype which has been on the ascendant in our culture in recent decades. We know what the mother side of this equation looks like. Let's describe The Orphan in more detail. The Orphan's main drive in life is to regain the "safety" they were deprived in childhood and that is exactly what The Devouring Mother will promise although not in the interests of securing genuine safety but in the interests of keeping The Orphan dependent. The Orphan's shadow traits – desire for illusory safety, insecurity, anxiety, apocalyptic fantasies, victimhood and blaming others for its own problems - have all been at the core of corona. The latter trait maps effortlessly onto both the mandatory mask and the vaccine issues which are primarily justified as being things other people must do to ensure the safety of The Orphan. Of course, this has no basis in science. We know masks don't work and we are now being told that, unlike practically every other vaccine, the corona vaccines do not prevent infection. Ergo, they don't work either. None of that matters in this case because it is not actual safety that The Orphan in shadow form desires but the illusion of safety. That's why it's not uncommon to hear the idea that we won't be safe til everybody has taken the vaccine. It's a complete fantasy but it's a fantasy specifically tailored to The Orphans.

However, it goes further than this. The Orphan in its shadow form doesn't merely require safety, it likes to use its feigned powerlessness to control others in much the same way that The Devouring Mother use emotional manipulation to wield control. I saw a random clip in mid-2021 where US politician, Ted Cruz, was asked by a journalist at a press conference to wear a mask because it would make the reporter "feel better". That's a prime example of The Orphan at work. If it was just about personal safety, The Orphan could wear a mask and take the vaccine and feel safe. That is not good enough, though. Everybody must wear a mask, everybody must take the vaccine and everybody must stay at home. The Devouring Mother wants those things to feed her will to power but it has been The Orphans among the public who have most fervently supported such measures. Just like The Devouring Mother's pretence of protecting her child hides deeper shadow desires, so The Orphan's pretence of powerlessness hides the desire to make others act on its behalf. The desire for special treatment is the primary addiction of The Orphan. If that special treatment involves overturning an entire society and coercing others into doing things that make no sense, that is of no concern. In fact, the more outlandish the special treatment, the better. It is also noteworthy that, at time of writing, some governments have already started declaring that the vaccinated will receive special treatment by being able to do things that the unvaccinated will not. This is a policy aimed squarely at The Orphans. All this explains why there has been a sizeable section of the public for whom it is not an exaggeration to say that they have been exhilarated by the corona event. They are The Orphans living out the ultimate Orphan fantasy of having the entire world rearranged in the name of *safety*. The Orphans are the Branch Covidian True Believers in the cult of corona, the ones who have actually been happy to have been locked up at home and even happier that everybody else got locked up too. We all became Orphans whether willingly or unwillingly in March 2020. We too were supposed to be defenceless against the virus and to need to be saved, a ridiculous claim when you look at the science, but the truth does not matter when archetypes are involved. Being returned to the symbolic safety of the home is exactly what The Orphan archetype desires and so the lockdowns were a perfect fit for both The Devouring Mother and The Orphan.

The Orphan in its shadow form desires to be rescued. Boris Johnson got up in the British parliament last year and announced "We can hear the toot of the scientific cavalry coming over the hill". The scientific soldiers were coming to the rescue. The doctors and nurses were going to save us too. Earlier in 2020, it had become the thing to do in Britain to go outside at a certain time of the day and cheer for the NHS. Doctors and nurses were the heroes all of a sudden. So too the scientists. At the Wimbledon tennis tournament in 2021, the crowd applauded the woman who had helped design the Astra Zeneca vaccine. We needed saving and the doctors, nurses and scientists were the ones to do it. It is both ironic and synchronistic that the official line at the start of corona was that the public needed to band together to "save the health system". We needed to save the experts who were going to save us. There's been an awful lot of saving going on and most of it largely illusory. Of course, it has all been for the benefit of The Orphans. The truth is, The Orphan must save itself. But its temptation is to let others do it. It can easily slip into a self-destructive mode where it will hurt both itself and others in order to avoid the challenge of individuation. When confronted with that challenge, The Orphan will lash out against those attempting to help it by telling it the truth. We have also seen that behaviour on display during corona. All dissenting expert voices have been silenced; a very strange thing given it was supposed to be the experts who would save us. The True Believers have had no problem dismissing the advice of people such as Luc Montagnier and Professor Bhakdi. We have even had the absurd situation where the very inventor of the mRNA vaccine, Robert Malone, has spoken out against the vaccination program only to be de-platformed from at least one social media site. The same thing happened to videos of the man who discovered Ivermectin. One would have thought we'd want to hear what such people have to say, but that hasn't been the case. The truth threatens the co-dependence relationship between The Devouring Mother and The Orphan. Anybody pointing out the truth can expect the wrath of both archetypes and that is exactly what we have seen in recent times starting with corona and then ramping up substantially with the Trump de-platforming. Seeing prominent figure de-platformed is now a daily occurrence. People were de-platformed for suggesting the virus escaped the lab in Wuhan only for that story to later become the accepted narrative. It's got nothing to do with the search for truth. It is, in fact, the denial of truth, something that both The Devouring Mother and The Orphan need in order to protect their relationship of co-dependence.

Perhaps the ultimate manifestation of The Orphan can be seen in the concept of *safe spaces*. As we have already seen, The Orphan primarily seeks safety and what better place to find it than a safe space. The safe space movement goes hand-in-hand with the victimhood ideology that has come to dominate in the universities and corporate culture and playing the victim is another archetypal facet of The Orphan in its shadow form. We will go into some detail later in the book about how Jordan Peterson left college campuses and took up the role of leader of the rebellious children preaching a gospel of personal responsibility, accountability and truthfulness. It's not hard to see why that had to happen. Universities have been progressively weeding out people like Peterson for some time, especially in the humanities faculties. Peterson's message is completely incompatible with the woke politics of the modern campus with its dizzying array of victim groups. The woke ideology along with the safe space is the precise manifestation of The Orphan archetype in its shadow form. Remember that The Orphan archetype's mission is to return to a place of safety but it is something they must achieve for themselves. By letting others do it for them, they lapse into their shadow side of powerlessness and victimhood. Almost by definition, providing a safe space for The Orphan archetype is encouraging them to lapse into their shadow. But that is exactly what The Devouring Mother wants because The Orphan in their shadow side is exactly what The Devouring Mother needs for the co-dependence relationship she seeks. Thus, the woke ideology, the victimhood and the safe spaces have all been encouraged and facilitated by the establishment. The game of playing the victim has taken some ridiculous forms with even the most privileged celebrities in the world now regularly claiming to be victims. Meanwhile, the safe spaces have been primarily located on college campuses, the very place where people go to graduate into adult life as fully educated members of society. In the 60s, university campuses were places of genuine education and genuine rebellion against the status quo. Not anymore. The woke ideology of university campuses is shared by the marketing department of every major corporation as well as Hollywood and the mainstream media. The Orphan in shadow form loves to play the victim and woke ideology allows it to do just that while being enabled by The Devouring Mother. The woke ideology and the safe spaces are there to feed The Orphan's shadow side and prevent it from attaining autonomy. The Orphans will graduate into a world of salary class *bullshit jobs* where autonomy and independent thinking are the exact opposite of what is required and so the education system is matched to the world which its students will enter.

It's worth spending some time now to go into more detail on this point as this will also lay the foundations for understanding the rebellious children in the next chapter. The rise of the woke ideology goes hand in hand with the rise of bullshit jobs, almost all of which are found in the salary class and require a university education to attain. These fit The Devouring Mother-Orphan relationship because, by definition, a bullshit job is not a *real* job. Because it's not a real job, the person who works in a bullshit job is denied genuine economic autonomy and economic autonomy is a key part of becoming an adult in any society. This is why the majority of the Branch Covidian True Believers have come from the salary class. In order to understand why this is so we need to zoom out and look at the nature of bureaucracy, the rise of corporations and the proliferation of bullshit jobs in the West in recent decades. We can then see how it ties in with The Orphan archetype's lack of economic independence.

Bullshit Jobs and the Loss of Economic Autonomy

Bureaucracies are great for building bridges or shipping things from A to B. They are, as a general rule, not so good at dealing with human beings for the reason that they are apt to treat human beings as objects. If, as Immanuel Kant said, man is always to be treated as an end in himself and never as a means, bureaucracies have a nasty habit of doing the latter. This is due to a phenomenon known as Goal Displacement. Bureaucracies might begin with an explicit mission to serve the interests of the customer but they quickly come to serve their own interests and treat the customer as a means to those interests. In a free market, if a company stops serving the interests of its customers, it will go out of business. But monopolistic or near monopolistic corporations and government bureaucracies do not have competition and so these are the most likely organisational type to treat people as mere objects. The mindset is captured beautifully in W H Auden's poem "The Unknown Citizen".

Was he free? Was he happy? The question is absurd:
Had anything been wrong, we should certainly have heard.

Bureaucracies see you through their own tiny lens and are completely unconcerned with you as a person. Anybody who has had to deal with a government department to achieve some trivial task only to be thwarted by pointless rules knows what it is like to be on the receiving end of Goal Displacement. The rules are there to serve the bureaucracy and not the customer. That's the first way in which bureaucracies go wrong and it's this that Kafka was chiefly concerned with i.e. the propensity of bureaucracies to treat humans as mere objects. Perhaps the ultimate expression of that can be found at the concentration camps where the Nazi bureaucracy kept immaculate administrative records of the people they were sending to their death.

Another way in which bureaucracies go wrong is when they get too much power and attempt to apply rules to inherently complex domains. Bureaucracies run on rules. It was this rule following behaviour which was initially seen as the strength of a bureaucracy. That might be true in mechanistic domains but it is not true in domains where there is inherent complexity. We have seen exactly this kind of problem in numerous ways during corona. The traditional strength of western societies has been to have a robust and autonomous (there's that word again) professional class to act as a buffer against government overreach. As we saw in the last chapter, during corona we have seen the medical professionals disintermediated by public health bureaucracies including being dictated to about what treatments to use rather than allowing doctors to do their job of finding the most effective treatments based on observation of actual patients. The flip side of that has been to demand acquiescence (there's that word again too) to the vaccine. In most western countries, nurses and doctors have been explicitly warned by their professional bodies not to speak out against the vaccine. To do so is to risk losing your career. Similarly, alternative treatments such as ivermectin have been ruled out despite the fact that a number of doctors have found them to work. In the normal course of events, where the side effects of a treatment or vaccine are well known, a doctor would be able to recommend to individual patients what was the best course of action based on the patient's profile. With corona, doctors have been sidelined and the whole thing is being run out of the bureaucracy which can only operate according to rules with all the clumsiness and confusion that causes. The skilled professionals have been replaced by bureaucrats in a process that James C. Scott outlined in his excellent book "Seeing Like a State". As described in that book, literally tens of millions of people died in the 20th century from giving bureaucracies too much power in this fashion. That's the second problem with bureaucracies.

The third problem is the psychological harm done to those who work in them. I can vouch for this from direct experience having briefly worked in a government bureaucracy. Mental health issues are a real problem. A number of HR departments in such organisations have responded by installing yoga rooms, chill out spaces, sleep cubicles and other token solutions but the underlying problem is the job itself. Such jobs cause real psychological damage. The reference to Kafka is relevant but the nature of the trauma has a different origin to what Kafka was describing. These jobs, the psychological effects of them and the organisational dynamics in bureaucracies which give rise to them have been described very succinctly by David Graeber with his concept of bullshit jobs.

> *To recap: what I am calling "bullshit jobs" are jobs that are primarily or entirely made up of tasks that the person doing that job considers to be pointless, unnecessary, or even pernicious. Jobs that, were they to disappear, would make no difference whatsoever. Above all, these are jobs that the holders themselves feel should not exist.*

Bullshit jobs cause real psychological trauma but, more importantly for an understanding of our current cultural malaise, they might make up perhaps 40% of the total jobs in western nations at the moment. Our hysterical overreaction to corona must have a source somewhere and one of the sources is surely the latent trauma caused by bullshit jobs. This is especially true because it has been the salary class that has been most hysterical about corona and it's also the salary class that works the lion's share of the bullshit jobs. In his book, Graeber does a good job of explaining how bureaucracies create bullshit jobs all by themselves due to politicking and internal dynamics. However, I think he misses the main cause of the rise of bullshit jobs and it's worth sketching out that history so we can understand why we got to where we are today.

The most important fact which explains why we have bullshit jobs is that industrial societies have been in massive economic surplus for more than a century. We have too much of everything. This is noticeable in the burgeoning waistlines of the citizens of western nations. It can be seen in the rise of the McMansion. It can be seen in storage companies who offer us a place to leave our stuff cos apparently our McMansions don't have enough room for it all. Marie Kondo owes her living to the fact that we have too much stuff and need somebody to tell us what to do with it. More important though is the way we got so much stuff. We got it by having machines do the work. Industrialisation always created unemployment right from the start. The standard wisdom states that the newly unemployed simply go on to better jobs. All those unemployed miners become factory workers and when the factory jobs disappear they all become software engineers until eventually everybody in society will be the CEO of a company living in a mansion and sailing their yacht to the Bahamas every summer. What happened in reality is that we eventually automated our way into a situation where there was a shortage of jobs that produce things of real value. But we still needed to have jobs because having a job is one of the foundational elements of our culture. That's where bullshit jobs came along to fill the void.

One way to understand this is to think about how it could have been different. In his brilliant 1932 essay, "In Praise of Idleness", Bertrand Russell makes the case that society should be organised in such a way that we all have to work as little as possible. That's right, the 4 hour work week is not a new idea. That this *could* be done was shown during WW1 when essentially the entire economies of European nations were centralised around the war effort. The bureaucracy turned out to be quite capable of organising boots, uniforms, helmets, guns, food and medicine for the soldiers during the war. Russell and others reasoned that it could provide shoes, clothes, household products, food and medicine for citizens during the peace. Moreover, if this was done, the amount of work required of citizens would be negligible. We could all do a few hours work a week and spend the rest of the time pursuing truth and beauty. I think there's all kinds of psychological and social reasons why that vision doesn't work but it does make logical sense. We could (probably) still do it today if we wanted to, but we have taken a very different route. In the immediate aftermath of WW2, western nations still had a relatively small number of bullshit jobs. There was a large manufacturing base and many jobs for clerks, office administrators, bookkeepers and the like. At the same time, the consumer economy kicked into gear and the advertising industry worked to increase the demand for products which helped create jobs to make those products. This created a long period of stability all the way into the 1970s when several things happened to spoil the party and caused the number of bullshit jobs to explode.

Firstly, there were the oil shocks and the associated stagflation of the 70s. Secondly, globalisation began and the west started offshoring manufacturing jobs to Japan and South Korea. Thirdly, the computer revolution began automating away many of the clerical and administrative jobs. The result of these three developments was that a huge chunk of steady, reliable, dependable work was lost. But the most important thing about that work was that it was valuable. This doesn't mean the jobs were easy or exciting or high status. It just means they had inherent value. Even a miner toiling away at back breaking work each day can point to a product that is of value that he or she helped to create. Having a job which creates something of actual value is intrinsically satisfying but we shipped those jobs overseas. In 2000, China was allowed into the WTO and the internet caused even more real jobs to be lost. All this led to the situation we are in now where, according to Graeber, 40% of jobs in western nations are bullshit jobs.

Let's look at the difference between a real job and a bullshit job. Let's say you were a bookkeeper for a manufacturing company in the 1950s. Your job had a real reason to exist and tangible outputs that were required. Thus, your performance could be judged objectively. You either balanced the accounts or you didn't. You either did the Thursday pay run or you didn't. You either got the tax files right or you didn't. This objectivity gave you a certain level of autonomy because your performance was straightforward to evaluate and couldn't be easily fudged for political reasons. Such objective criteria don't exist in a bullshit job. What exists instead is politics and ideology. With a real job, you can get better over time and take pride and satisfaction in improving your skills. With a bullshit job, it's just an endless parade of political manoeuvrings. This is another factor behind all the woke ideology that comes out of universities and corporations these days. It's all there to sort out the internal politics of bullshit jobs. Note that practically every story about some crime against woke-ism features somebody getting sacked. Getting or losing a bullshit job is not based on performance but on fealty to the ideology.

Now that we know what a bullshit job is and why they are there, the final piece of the puzzle is to ask why bureaucracies feature so many bullshit jobs. The answer is simply that bureaucracies lend themselves to expansion. This is actually a strength of a bureaucracy; it scales easily and allows things like bridges and damns, which require a large amount of coordinated labour, to be built. But, in a society where there are not enough jobs that create value to go around, bureaucracies can just as easily expand by creating bullshit jobs. It's not hard to see why this is the case. A small business almost never creates a bullshit job because the money to hire any new employee comes directly out of the owner's pocket and the owner has every incentive not to spend that money if they get no return. In a bureaucracy, on the other hand, you're spending other peoples' money. And what you're buying as an ambitious middle manager is political power; new employees who will be faithful to you. This is why bureaucracies have become synonymous with bullshit jobs in the modern world. We needed to create jobs and we didn't have enough good jobs to go around, so we created bullshit jobs and the bureaucracy is the most efficient organisational form for doing so. That is also part of the reason why corporations and government have become so intertwined. Politicians promised voters they would create jobs and corporations were there to help. The fact that the jobs are bullshit is of secondary importance.

Because bullshit jobs cause psychological distress, many modern bureaucracies have become little more than trauma factories. In mid-2021, I saw a random social media post by a salary class woman who was "terrified" that things were about to go back to normal. What she meant was, she was going to have to go back to her office with all the psychological problems that go with it. The call for a "new normal" was, I think, a thinly veiled cry for help from such people. What they really need is a proper job. People need to know they are creating value of some kind and they need this value to be socially recognised by others. A social hierarchy based on this creation of value is inherently stable. But a social hierarchy based on bullshit jobs is not. The rise of bullshit jobs has given our society a paranoid and anxious disposition and it is here that we come full circle and link back to The Orphan archetype because The Orphan's problem is exactly that paranoia, that feeling of anxiety that comes from not standing on firm ground. Back in the 1990s, anti-globalisation campaigners warned of exactly this outcome. One of the most eloquent of them was Sir James Goldsmith who noted that the economy must work for society, not the other way around. We should be first and foremost concerned with creating meaningful work or, in the absence of that, follow Bertrand Russell's advice and find something else that is meaningful to do. Instead, we prioritised the economy. More specifically, we prioritised the financial interests of certain groups in society over the welfare of the broader public. This is where we also link back to The Devouring Mother because fulfilling her own needs and not the interests of her children is exactly her problem; unrestrained will to power. Just like a good Devouring Mother, the corporations who benefit from globalisation hide their real intentions behind a façade of compassion. They run on ideology which represents a form of emotional manipulation and gaslighting. To know that the job you are working in creates no value while having to display fealty to irrelevant ideological dogmas is disorienting and confusing. It doesn't help that the dogma itself is internally inconsistent. The woke ideology claims to be all about inclusiveness and diversity but go to work and show your support for Trump and you'll soon find out how inclusive the place is and how much diversity of political opinion is tolerated. Part of learning to do a bullshit job is to deal with such paradoxes and one of the easiest ways to deal with them is to pretend they don't exist. That is why the truth becomes so explosive for such people. This is the path of The Orphan who acquiesces. You become economically co-dependent on The Devouring Mother in the form of the corporation, trapped in a gaslighting relationship where you are initially unable to speak truth and eventually unable to deal with it at all. The viciousness of the woke ideology is the viciousness of The Orphans indulging in the shadow side of the archetype, simultaneously playing the victim while engaging in predatory behaviour towards others. All of this is egged on by The Devouring Mother who knows that the children arguing amongst themselves will not achieve independence and will remain permanently dependent on the monthly salary that arrives no matter how much actual work got done or value created. That monthly salary is itself an illusion of security for The Orphan. It seems so regular and dependable while it lasts. But skills in navigating the cutthroat world of corporate politics are not readily transferable outside the corporation. Having acquiesced once, it becomes harder and harder to break out of the web one has spun for oneself.

When the average acquiescent child is not working in a salary class bullshit job, they are fulfilling their other main societal role which is that of the consumer. The nature of this consumption has also changed substantially in the last couple of decades with the advent of the internet. Alongside pay tv and then the various streaming services such as Netflix, the number of options for electronic entertainment has exploded all of which has had the effect of keeping people in their homes. I noted in The Plague Story that the increased anxiety towards death in our culture came from increasing urbanisation and the subsequent lack of exposure the average person had to "nature" in the broadest sense of the word. It is this trend towards urbanisation in bullshit jobs, consumerism and electronic entertainment which produces The Orphan archetype. The lack of autonomy in the workplace is complemented by a lack of self-sufficiency that comes from consumerism. There's a passage in Robert Pirsig's *Zen and the Art of Motorcycle Maintenance* where he talks about the anxiety that comes from not being able to fix things, whether it be a repairing a motorcycle or stopping a tap from leaking. This anxiety is exactly The Orphan's trait of powerlessness and it is stereotypical of the modern consumer in a world where consumer items are designed to be thrown away (planned obsolescence) and deliberately made too complex to be repaired and maintained by the average person (as in most modern cars). Pirsig described this as the feeling of being surrounded by things you are unable to control because you don't know how they work. That word "control" has been around a lot during corona. It wasn't so much that a virus was spreading, it was that the virus was "out of control". This feeling of not being in control, not being able to fix things, not being able to create real wealth represents an overall lack of economic autonomy. That was bad enough but it was tolerable while the feeling of growing one's wealth was still present. But even that is now disappearing. The consumer economy has been increasingly financed by debt in the last couple of decades. In fact, the whole economic system has slowly become debt-based, a sign that it no longer pays for it itself. Of course, corona has only added more debt to an already unsustainable pile. In relation to The Orphan's specifically, they have been required to accrue enormous student loans for entry into the game of the salary class. These are predatory by their very nature and serve to trap unwitting students who must chase high-paying, high-status jobs to avoid falling out of the system altogether as student loans cannot even be cancelled by bankruptcy in the US. If The Orphan's task is to strive for a modicum of independence, the system prevents this from happening. It is now little more than debt bondage that encourages The Orphan's shadow behaviour. The feelings of victimhood and powerlessness are the shadow side of The Orphan and are actually a very accurate description of their position in modern society, but they are trapped. The predatory nature of the system, the financial co-dependence that is built into it and the ideological gaslighting that is at the centre of it are all The Devouring Mother at play. The Orphan who acquiesces will find themselves in the shadow side projecting their genuine insecurities onto the world but The Devouring Mother is there to ensure these are projected not at her where they belong but against the other side of the equation: the rebellious children. It is to the rebellious children that we will turn in the next chapter.

Chapter 3: The Rebellious Children

In late January of 2020, Boris Johnson finally got the UK across the finish line as the country withdrew from the EU bringing to a close the formalities of the process that had begun with the Brexit referendum in mid-2016. Donald Trump, who had won the US election in November 2016, was entering the final year of his term having been impeached a few weeks earlier by the US House of Representatives over something to do with the Ukraine (does it really matter what?). The impeachment came on the back of three years of seemingly the entire US establishment attempting to pin the cause for Trump's victory on what turned out to be fictitious collusion with Russia. In early January 2020, Jordan Peterson travelled to Russia. The Canadian professor of psychology, who had shot to superstardom in 2016 (are we sensing a pattern?), had become addicted to prescription medication and, apparently not being able to find appropriate treatment in North America, had decided to go to Moscow for help. On arrival, he was diagnosed with having pneumonia. It was only a week or two prior that an apparently unusual cluster of pneumonia cases had broken out to the east in Wuhan, China. While Peterson was lying in an induced coma, the beginnings of the event that was to overturn the world were taking shape; the corona event. All three men in question – Johnson, Trump and Peterson – would test positive to corona during 2020. Johnson wound up in hospital. Peterson was already in hospital, this time in Serbia. According to his daughter's report, his corona symptoms were mild but that had not stopped doctors "putting him on everything", not a little ironic for a man who had just spent six months trying to get off medication. Trump would famously test positive in the last few weeks of the presidential election campaign, although he was clearly one of the many asymptomatic "cases" of corona. He too went to hospital but that was purely for show. In typical Trump fashion, he took the opportunity in the middle of his visit to have a car ride outside to smile and wave to adoring fans.

What unites Trump, Peterson and Johnson is not just a positive corona test. All three men were leaders of a revolt that had taken place in western culture beginning four years earlier. We have seen that there are two options available for the children of The Devouring Mother: to rebel or to acquiesce. It was in 2016 that the rebellious children found their voice. Trump, Peterson and Johnson were leaders of that rebellion. But the rebellion, or at least their leadership of it, seems to have come to an end in 2020. Trump lost the election and was also de-platformed from the social media sites he had so expertly used to launch himself to the presidency. Although not a spent force by any stretch, it's hard to see him becoming a contender again now that the establishment has found a way to silence him. Johnson held onto his job but the self-proclaimed libertarian led Britain into arguably the least libertarian period it had experienced in centuries. Peterson has joined the ranks of the public intellectuals who chose to sit out corona. The man who won fame and admiration for taking a stand against the petty tyranny of the wokeists in Canadian universities and who railed against the totalitarianism caused by communism apparently decided not to have an opinion as western societies themselves lurched towards authoritarianism. Having spent the first half of 2020 battling to get off medications and despite having already had the virus, Peterson announced in May 2021 that he was getting the vaccine because his "antibody levels appeared insufficient to prevent re-infection". The reaction of many of his fans was not one of approval, a fact which his enemies in the MSM took delight in pointing out.[1]

We have already seen how the corona event fits into the archetype of The Devouring Mother and The Orphan and how the relationship between the two has been ascendant in western society in the last few decades. Now we are going to add another piece to that historical context: the rise of the rebels. Corona represents the fightback of The Devouring Mother against three of her most rebellious children and their followers. If 2016 was the year when the rebels made their voices heard, 2020 was the year when the empire struck back. What will happen next is anybody's guess but for now we can explore the nature of this battle with particular reference to Peterson and Trump who best characterise the rebellious children and their fight for independence and autonomy. Both men won support by tapping into the latent dissatisfaction felt by a sizeable proportion of the population. That dissatisfaction is precisely the dissatisfaction felt by the child of The Devouring Mother. There were many such *children* looking for a way to rebel in 2016 and Trump and Peterson appeared on the scene to meet the demand. Let's take a look at each man in turn to see what they reveal about the nature of the rebellious children of The Devouring Mother.

Jordan Peterson

It is fitting that Jordan Peterson erupted from the modern university like Jonah being spat out of the belly of the beast. As we saw in the last chapter, universities these days have become nothing more than ideology factories which, in a perverted way, do provide appropriate training for those who are going to graduate into a world of salary class bullshit jobs where knowing how to play along with ideological power games is the main predictor of success. It is also fitting that Peterson is a professor of psychology. In the world of The Devouring Mother with its gaslighting and emotional manipulation, the children are in need of psychiatric counselling and here was a man who did that for a living. If the rebellious baby boomers found their escape valve in sex, drugs and rock'n'roll, a couple of generations later Peterson offers almost the exact opposite. In a world awash with porn, twenty-four hour "news" broadcasts, endless entertainment options, social media and information saturation, Peterson has offered meaning (his first book was called *Maps of Meaning*). He has described to a generation of young people who have been taught that the culture they live in is at best something to be corrected and at worst downright evil what exactly that culture was good for. Because that message is so vanishingly rare these days, Peterson became a kind of magnet for, among other things, the desire for gratitude. The standing ovations he received at the start (not just the end) of his speeches were a sign of that. Here was a man who surveyed western culture and said "it is good and here's why." His detractors accused him of being reactionary but that missed the point. His was a message that many people had simply never heard because, in the house of The Devouring Mother, every bit of praise hides a secret intent; an ulterior motive. Peterson had no ulterior motive, quite the opposite. He may have been ejected out of the belly of the modern university but, if I may be permitted a mixed metaphor, he was thrown straight into the frying pan of the modern culture wars. Alongside the usual torrent of online hatred that players in the culture war can expect, Peterson also put himself on the line in public. He had protestors at his speaking events. He had hysterical people screaming into his face on the street. That can't be a very fun way to spend your time but Peterson stood firm and in doing so his star continued to rise. Here was a man who stood for what he believed in. That symbol is what an awful lot of people were looking for and it also became a central part of Peterson's message to his followers. In a world filled with the endless gaslighting of The Devouring Mother, here was a rare gem of authenticity.

Peterson's message was not just authentic but authoritative. Not, however, in the way that The Devouring Mother's message is authoritative. The Devouring Mother demands submission. The gaslighting and propaganda asks not to be understood, internalised, reasoned about and discussed, it demands unthinking repetition and fealty. It also changes every other week because the point of it is not to be "true". It is not a means to the end of knowledge but a means to the end of power. For years the establishment media in the US banged on endlessly about

Trump and Russia then changed on a dime when Ukraine served their purposes better and when that was done it was all about corona. Now it will go back to being about race or climate change or whatever else does the job. The "authority" it wields issues from the ability to control the narrative. If the narrative is a complete and total lie, it simply does not matter. That's what makes it gaslighting; the ability to say what is patently untrue and have it accepted as truth. Peterson's authority is very different. He draws on equal parts biblical scholarship and science. In doing so, he combines the two primary sources of historical authority in western civilisation. It is an authority that stretches back over millennia. It is also the authority of common sense. One of the criticisms of Peterson is that he is long-winded; that he takes a hundred words to speak a basic truth that could have been said in a sentence. But that criticism also misses the point. Yes, Peterson is stating the obvious but there are a large number of people who want to hear the obvious. In a world where authority figures state blatant lies in public every day, the man who gets up and states the obvious truth is a revolutionary figure who challenges the power structure. That is what Peterson did. As the saying goes – knowledge is power. Teach a man to fish and you give him knowledge and thereby power and autonomy. In the house of The Devouring Mother, as we saw in the last chapter, you are not taught to fish. You are given a fish and then told you don't deserve it.

To a large extent, the rebellious children of The Devouring Mother chose Peterson. I don't mean that they consciously chose him. I mean it was subconscious. It was archetypal. As the saying goes "when the student is ready, the teacher will appear". Or perhaps we can rephrase that "when the Devouring Mother appears, the children get ready to rebel". But the teacher in this case was always there. Peterson had been delivering his lectures to students at the University of Toronto since 1998 and had been uploading those lectures to Youtube in the years prior to 2016. Like most university professors, he was active to some extent in the public discourse and was a guest on various intellectual programs during his tenure at the University of Toronto. But, it was a series of videos he posted in 2016 that finally propelled him into the spotlight.

In the videos he criticised a bill that was going through the parliament in Canada about gender pronouns. That is another synchronicity because the whole gender pronoun thing is one of the purest examples of a power game imposed as ideology; the kind of thing that has become more and more common recently. In challenging it, Peterson challenged The Devouring Mother directly but that was not the important part. No doubt there were thousands of videos floating around on the internet of people arguing against such measures. What was important was that the minions in the mainstream media decided to give Peterson some coverage and in so doing they brought him to the attention of the people who were desperately looking for a voice that *could* fight back against the ideology that was being imposed on them. Peterson's voice - authentic and authoritative - fitted the bill. Because Peterson already had a substantial amount of material online, those primarily young people and primarily young men had something firm to grasp onto and so began the ever quickening co-evolution of a leader with his audience. One of the advantages of social media and online communication channels, and this is something Trump also used to expert effect, is that they give real time feedback on how a message is received by an audience. They also allow global reach. Peterson was no longer addressing just a half full lecture theatre in Toronto, he was addressing the young people of the western world in general and he was able to gauge in real time what they wanted to hear. His best-selling book *12 Rules for Life* began as an internet site where he was able to judge from the audience response what they were looking for. What they were looking for were rules. The lawgiver has a strong symbolism in the collective unconscious. The lawgiver speaks with authority vested in him in some way. For Moses, and other prophets, it was vested by God. Peterson claimed his authority not from God directly but from the Bible and from modern science. By contrast, the faceless ideologues who grease the wheels of the modern propaganda machine do not claim authority from anywhere other than their ability to have their words splayed across screens. Thus, news reports are full of empty phrases like "experts say" or "scientists are increasingly finding...". A lot of modern media claims its authority from nothing more than what anonymous sources blurted out on twitter yesterday afternoon. Peterson claims his authority from his understanding of the ideas that have shaped western civilisation. In that way he became a genuine authority figure; a lawgiver. Hence the fact that his bestselling book is about *rules* for life. Two of the most famous of these rules were clean your bedroom and stand up straight (so that you can find a mate). Both of those are tailored to the male children of The Devouring Mother and represent the desire to become a full-fledged adult male in a society which desperately wants you to remain the eternally dependent child. That is why Peterson's message resonated most strongly with young men. He became a father figure on a global scale but it was a role he had to step into. His transition into it began in earnest in 2016 and has continued up to the present day. One can see it very clearly in the way he has changed his appearance during that time. Go back and have a look at Peterson in 2016. He was clean shaven and, if I may be so bold as to judge, sloppily dressed. A couple of years later he was giving speeches and doing media performances in suit and tie with a well-manicured grey beard complemented by sharp hairstyling. If the clothes maketh the man, the man was now a boss.

It's in the rise of Peterson and Trump as the opposition to The Devouring Mother that we first really see the mother for what she is. She has been on the ascendant for decades but it wasn't until 2016 that her dominance became obvious. It wasn't until the opposition formed itself that we could see what it was trying to oppose. Peterson as lawgiver speaks in the stern, dour tone of an old protestant pastor. His message is one of duty over happiness, of striving against difficulty and triumph in self overcoming and, perhaps most importantly in the world of endless gaslighting, of speaking the truth. He tells his followers that they are not perfect little angels who have been corrupted by the big bad world. Rather, they are just as capable as anyone of perpetrating evil. The battle between good and evil is within them just as much as without. "I am a man and nothing human is foreign to me," said Montaigne and Peterson would agree. This is in stark contrast to the prevailing ideology of The Devouring Mother who tells her acquiescent children they *are* perfect little angels. They don't need to do anything to be happy. Rather, happiness is being withheld from them by forces outside themselves. As a psychologist and Jungian scholar, Peterson would know that this is The Orphan in its shadow form. Both The Devouring Mother and her acquiescent children are projecting the shadow. To the extent that the forces keeping them dissatisfied are the other people in society, the ideology of The Devouring Mother translates into the perfect vehicle for turning the population (the children) against each other and that is how it all plays out politically. Peterson was on the receiving end of that treatment when he pulled on his gloves and stepped into ring of the culture wars. It is the world that must change, not you. So speaks The Devouring Mother to her acquiescent children. It is you that must change, says Peterson to the rebellious children. Pull yourself together, Bucko. Start by cleaning your room. Then try and find a mate and a place in the world. Once you've got yourself sorted out, you can worry about society. This message of personal development and personal responsibility was dynamite precisely because it threatened the existing order which had slowly built up over decades; the order of The Devouring Mother preventing her children from achieving autonomy. One interesting random statement I saw in relation to Peterson was: "Jordan Peterson could never have happened in the 90s". I think that's right. The 90s, of course, was when globalisation kicked into hyperdrive and the middle class in the USA and large parts of Europe was thrown under the bus. It is when the future Jordan Peterson followers were born. They were born into a world of consumerism and bullshit jobs and it is from that world that they seek escape. That is what Peterson offered.

Those are the broad outlines of how Peterson rose to fame channelling the support of the rebellious children and directly confronting the gaslighting and ideological-emotional manipulation that has been at the core of The Devouring Mother's ascendancy in recent decades. As we know, Peterson was laid low in late 2019 and the first half of 2020. What was it that brought Peterson undone? Prescription medication. The modern medical industry. I suppose you could argue that this is just coincidence, but we know better by now. It's a synchronicity. It's

The Devouring Mother in her Munchausen by Proxy form as described in Chapter 1. Prescription medication has, of course, claimed an enormous number of lives in North America in recent decades. To give two examples that have personal relevance for me as I am a huge fan of both their music. Firstly, Chris Cornell, one of the all-time great rock singers known best for his work with Soundgarden, died in a hotel room in 2017. The cause of death was officially suicide but Cornell had no less than five different prescription medications in his system at the time. His widow sued Cornell's doctor for prescribing the medications that she believed caused her husband's death and the doctor settled out of court. Secondly, Prince, one of the all-time great electric guitarists alongside his pop music career, died in his home of an overdose of fentanyl in 2016. Fentanyl is the drug that has been at the centre of the opioid crisis in the US. A couple of people close to the musician had tried to organise to get him into a similar program of rehab that Peterson would go through in 2020 but they did not get it organised in time to prevent his death. Numerous similar cases could no doubt be found for both famous and non-famous people. What is strange in Peterson's case is that he is on the record pointing out exactly these issues with the medical system in North America. His journey to eastern Europe to seek treatment for his own problems speaks to a deep distrust of that system and symbolically represents him fleeing from The Devouring Mother in order to get better. This is all in keeping with the Munchausen by Proxy archetype. One would have expected him to bring that perspective to bear directly on the corona event. Instead, he acquiesced. As noted above, this acquiescence has brought him into conflict with his followers who, I think rightly, expected him to speak out against what has happened. Corona should have been right up his alley. His failure to speak has meant that people looking for a dissenting voice failed to get one. To the extent that corona represents The Devouring Mother fighting back against her rebellious children, this is a substantial setback. The voices of the rebellious children were silenced. What that means for Peterson in the years ahead will be a very interesting one to watch. Will his failure mean the rebellious children will start looking for another leader? Or will his failure of leadership bring an end to the movement as a whole?

Trump

So much has already been written about the Trump phenomenon and I do not intend to add much here except to do a lightning overview of how Trump fits into The Devouring Mother – rebellious child relationship. It barely needs saying that Trump was a rebel. He was a political outsider who took on the entire US establishment and won. In doing so, he created a movement that was bigger than Peterson's. It was Michael Moore of all people who most concisely summed up that movement when he described Trump as a human Molotov cocktail that his supporters wanted to throw into the system. The rebellious children who supported Trump were not just the young people, they were everybody who had been thrown under the bus as globalisation that had kicked into hyperdrive in the 90s. For them, "Make America Great Again" had a tangible resonance because they had seen with their own eyes the destruction wrought on the places where they lived (mostly in flyover country). Trump was offering to turn that around. His opponent in the election was the wife of the President who started the whole process. That would have been bad enough, but now she showed up again twenty years later and, rather than ask for atonement or offer an apology, she simply looked down her nose at them. Again, Michael Moore hit the mark in saying "The last thing you want to do is wag your finger, your adult finger, at these millennials. They're upset about the whole thing. They're upset about the world that's been handed to them." Your "adult" finger? I think we can safely translate that as your "Devouring Mother finger" because that's what Hillary Clinton was waving at Trump supporters and not just the millennials. Of course, she labelled them the "deplorables" and in so doing gave a name to the group and inadvertently helped to catalyse the movement which had been forming right under her nose and to which she seemed completely oblivious. That movement was the rebellious children and Clinton was their Devouring Mother. With the tag "deplorable" she did not merely dismiss them but disowned them. That is not behaviour befitting somebody running for president. Although you may criticise the other side, ultimately you hope to be elected and when you are president you are supposed to at least pretend to govern for everybody. But Clinton couldn't hide her contempt. Her behaviour was not befitting a presidential candidate but it was befitting a Devouring Mother who will happily disown her rebellious children. The truth is, the deplorables had already been disowned decades earlier and it was just now they were fighting back. In his victory speech at the Republican convention, Trump said "I am your voice". That was right. He was the voice of the rebellious children who had coalesced behind him into an open rebellion against the status quo in politics. Much like Peterson had modified himself into the lawgiver in a process of co-evolution with his audience, so Trump modified himself as he tailored his message in response to whatever got the most applause at his rallies. This gave rise to such phrases as "drain the swamp". Two others were also notable – "lock her up" and "crooked Hillary". Clinton, the wife of the man who kicked globalisation into overdrive, a creature of the swamp and, most crucially of all, the very personification in tone of voice and attitude of The Devouring Mother.

Everybody remembers Trump's campaign slogan which has become part of the culture now. Fewer will remember Clinton's but it is another symbol that links her to The Devouring Mother archetype - "I'm with her". This is a statement of allegiance pure and simple. It denotes no political content, no notion of what she will do for the nation or what she will deliver to you the voter. In it there is no hint whatsoever as to what the Clinton campaign stood for other than to get her elected. It is a slogan for the acquiescent children. The Devouring Mother asks only for submission and allegiance and this precisely what "I'm with her" entails. By contrast, *Make America Great Again* is a goal and a mission. Something is wrong in the world and by voting for Trump you can make it right. Like Peterson, this phrase draws on history. In order to understand what it means, you must know what America was like when it was great, what has gone wrong since and what needs to be done to get it back. It is, of course, the same slogan Reagan used. In this way, Trump aligned himself with history. Just like with Peterson, the rebellious children were looking to identify what their tradition was and to ground themselves in it. In politics, that tradition is the democratic nation state and so it is fitting that *Make America Great Again* explicitly foregrounds the nation. "I'm with her" is not about the nation, it's about *her* and you really got the impression from Clinton that she thought this was enough. That she *deserved* to be elected president just because of who she was. It is no small irony that the media attempted to present things in exactly the opposite way. Trump was supposed to be the vainglorious one only running for President to boost his ego while Clinton was the cool, experienced insider who knew how to work the system and would keep it running smoothly. But the rebellious children did not want the system to run smoothly anymore. It had been running them smoothly into the ground for decades and they had had enough. They wanted somebody to throw a spanner in the works and Trump knew how to portray himself as the man for the job.

Four years later, it all came to an end in the Capitol protest, an event as surreal as the rest of the Trump presidency. I don't know what to make of it on a factual level and from the other side of the world I wouldn't like to judge. Symbolically, it works. Trump had brought the rebellious children to the seat of power to air their grievances. Of course, the whole thing was deeply weird and didn't make much logical sense and that is also fitting of archetypal occurrences. One of the most memorable photos of the occasion was the man dressed in the horns and animal fur hat. I have no idea what archetype he was embodying but he certainly represented the fact that the event was mostly taking place down in the depths of the psyche and scarcely at all in the rational mind. In any case, it was this event which finally gave the establishment an excuse to de-platform Trump and that more than anything characterised his defeat. The rebellious child had been grounded, perhaps permanently.

Much more could be said about all this, but I think that overview suffices for our purposes. What's left to explain is how corona brought the Trump train to a sudden stop. I suspect that Trump knew what he was up against symbolically when corona kicked off. In early February he tweeted that it was "just the flu", a statement which has turned out to be factually correct in the overwhelming majority of cases. But, ultimately, he had to give in. The entire establishment, which had been running the Russia angle against him for three years, had cottoned on to what could be done with the corona story. He did the next best thing which was to push the idea of heroic science in the form of the vaccine but it was never something he really believed in and it showed. It is not coincidental that this has also been Peterson's position on corona; a kind of acceptance of "science". Invoking the authority of science works just as well in politics as in the culture wars. The problem these days is that institutionalised science has been corrupted. In one of those ironies that history regularly throws up, that the man who invented the PCR which was misused to generate the corona event, Kary Mullis, was on record decades earlier pointing out that institutionalised science was corrupt. He also had some, shall we politely say, unflattering things to say about a certain man named Fauci, the very man Trump found himself having to put in charge of the corona response. In doing so, he handed over power to The Devouring Mother. I believe it was the first time in his presidency where he lost a battle on the symbolic level. However, he did not go down without a fight. In the last weeks of the election campaign, Trump tested positive to corona. Although clearly asymptomatic, he went to hospital for a few days. On his release, Trump told the people not to live in fear of the virus. "Don't let it dominate your life", he said. He could have been talking about The Devouring Mother directly.

It was notable that at Trump election rallies later in the year the crowd was chanting "fire Fauci". This was well before the lab leak story went mainstream. Trump himself had won in 2016 by promising to dismantle Obamacare, a prime example of the corruption in the medical system. The rebellious children had been at the pointy end of all this corruption for a long time. They knew the score just like Peterson's supporters who have spoken out against his support of the vaccine also know the score. At least some of the rebellious children also want to throw a Molotov cocktail into the corrupt system of institutionalised medicine and science but both Trump and Peterson were unwilling or unable to lead them there. Perhaps that's because they also know that this represents a genuine split in their supporter base. Appeals to "science" still cut across the political divide. In Trump's case, he chose the path he thought was least damaging politically. He was probably right but that did not stop him from losing. Trump even decided to throw his support behind the mask mandates which, as we will see in Chapter 5, was a big symbolic mistake. In any case, The Devouring Mother got her revenge. She seemed to know exactly the point at which to split the rebels in two and diminish their power. That point was the faith in "science".

It seems to have escaped the notice of most commentators that the Trump platform was in large part the promise of reversing the globalisation of the 90s. The jobs Trump promised he would return to America were exactly the jobs that had been lost to other countries in that time. The irony of this was that in the 90s it was the "left" who campaigned against globalisation. Twenty years later, it was the "right" promising to overturn it. That's a rapid change in political position. The meaning of the words "left" and "right in politics had flipped almost 180 degrees. This shifting of the meaning of words has been evident in other areas of society in the last twenty years. It is no coincidence that Jordan Peterson rose to fame in large part by pushing back against such semantic changes in the form of gender pronouns. During corona we have seen changes in the meaning of the word "case", "herd immunity", "vaccine" and even the very concept of "disease". The state now reserves the right to pronounce you diseased based on a test result instead of on symptoms. All that has changed markedly even from the first SARS event back in 2003. What the rebellious children were looking for was somebody to make sense of all this change and one of the best ways to do that is to reach back into history. This explains the appeal of Peterson whose lectures of biblical stories provide a framework for understanding (a map of meaning in Peterson's language) for a generation struggling with the confusion of navigating even the basic meaning of words used in public discourse. Language is power, said Peterson. Being able to speak and write clearly is the same as being able to think clearly and thereby to see through the fog of the modern culture wars and the gaslighting of The Devouring Mother. By reaching back into the past, Peterson was able to make sense of the present. Trump's *Make America Great Again* is the same idea. It grounds the present in the past. By contrast, the woke ideology problematises the past. The underlying assumption is that the past is holding us back. But this is also just projecting the shadow. The acquiescent children are as much at sea as the rebellious children. They suffer even more from the ever-changing meaning of words because their entire social position is tied to ensuring they know which words are the right ones to say at any given time. The punishment for failure on this score is to be de-platformed and not just from your social media account. The anxiety of The Orphan is magnified by the miasma of an ever-changing ideology. The desire to revert to a simpler past is perfectly understandable. Both Peterson and Trump were mocked for promising as much. We can't possibly "go backwards", it was said. But this misses the point. When you take the wrong pathway, it's perfectly logical to go back and find the right one. Of course, there is no right and wrong in these matters. But there is the obvious psychological problems caused by a too rapid change in society. The rebellious children seek to address the problem by re-establishing a link to the past. They want to stand on firm ground. The Devouring Mother wants them to remain unsure. Hence the unresolved tension of the last half a decade.

Chapter 4: How Dare You

We have now sketched out the primary dynamics involved in The Devouring Mother archetype. We have seen the core relationship between the mother and the acquiescent child - aka The Orphan in its shadow form. And we saw in the last chapter that the rebellious children found their voice in 2016 through the Trump and Brexit votes and the emergence of Jordan Peterson. This occurred exactly one generation after globalisation went into hyperdrive and threw much of the western middle class under the bus. The Trump victory, like the Brexit one, represented a huge shock to the political system. It was the first time the public had explicitly rejected the ascendance of The Devouring Mother. The hysteria that followed those votes spoke to the psychic forces that were involved. These were not normal political victories and losses with the usual licking of the wounds and regrouping on the part of the defeated. Something much deeper was at stake and that something was the archetypes of The Devouring Mother and The Orphan. It was these archetypes which grasped onto the corona event turning it from what was, at worst, a middle of the road pandemic in the magnitude of the Hong Kong flu of 1968 and magnifying it psychologically and politically into the next Black Death.

With The Devouring Mother and The Orphan archetypes at hand, we can now make sense of a precursor phenomenon to corona and one that links the corona event to the climate change propaganda of recent times: the rise of Greta Thunberg. It is no coincidence that Thunberg emerged in the northern hemisphere summer of 2018 just after the Trump-Brexit rebellions. She emerged in response to them. But before we get into an archetypal analysis of Thunberg, it is important to understand a bit of historical context about the environmental movement which she has "led". Just like universities used to be sites of real rebellion back in the 60s and 70s, so the environmental movement at that time was a real grassroots enterprise that aimed for meaningful change in society. Like every grassroots movement, the environmentalists were initially concerned with tangible issues on the ground and they achieved some genuine wins by highlighting a number of obvious and easily fixed problems such as lead poisoning from petrol and paint. There's an interesting bit of Australian history that serves to illustrate what that looked like. Not many people know this, but the name of the political party The Greens came indirectly from Australia. Back in the 1970s, there were a series of so called "green bans" led by union leader Jack Mundey in New South Wales. The bans were applied to building projects that diminished the environmental or heritage value of whatever area the proposed development was in. Local members of the community would raise their concerns with the union who would then declare a green ban on the project. The person who would later found The Greens in Germany, Petra Kelly, happened to be visiting Sydney at the time of the green bans and used the moniker as the inspiration for the name of her new political party. That's what was called environmentalism in those days. It was a grassroots movement. Even at that early time, however, corruption was evident. Jack Mundey and his colleagues in NSW were sacked by a corrupt national union whose leader would later be found guilty of taking bribes from developers. That seemingly isolated incident was indicative of what happened to environmentalism in general. Like any movement, once the easy wins had been realised, the environmentalists continued to push for measures that were more costly to the status quo. It became in the interests of the establishment to buy them out and that is precisely what happened. Environmentalist leaders were either removed by force such as in Mundey's case or, more commonly, took up well paying positions on advisory boards or consulting to the marketing departments of corporations and government. As that happened, the real grassroots movement that represented the concerns of real people promptly disappeared in a puff of environmentally friendly smoke. What has been called "green" ever since is whatever suits vested interests including and especially the enormous infrastructure spending on so-called renewable energy. By the time 2018 rolled around, environmentalism was run through various NGOs which are simply fronts that hide the real financial and political interests at play. It was in this world that Greta Thunberg decided to skip school and protest alone in front of the Swedish parliament in Stockholm.

In the previous chapter I noted that Jordan Peterson's rise to fame was partly due to his authenticity. The same can certainly be said for Greta Thunberg. She's definitely one of a kind. There's no way some marketing department or paid political hacks could come up with somebody like a Thunberg. Also like Peterson, Thunberg's rise has been facilitated by social media but it is here that a crucial difference between the two reveals what has really been going on. Recall that Peterson had been putting his material online for some time and had built a small following in the years before 2016. His videos about the pronoun issue were picked up by mainstream media with the intention of holding him up as an example of everything that was wrong in the world and this brought him to the attention of the people who were looking for somebody to speak against the system. That gave his existing online channels a big boost and over the next years Peterson learned to use those channels to build his audience. Just like Trump, Peterson benefitted from the negative media coverage and used it to his advantage to become a leader of the rebellious children. The situation with Thunberg is completely different. In many ways, Thunberg is an inversion of Peterson. Peterson is a middle-aged male teacher and scholar. In 2018, Thunberg was a 15 year old schoolgirl. Old vs young. Adult vs child. Male vs female. Teacher vs student. If Peterson was leading the rebels, it would follow that Thunberg must be leading the establishment. However, Thunberg was herself supposed to be rebelling. After all, she was skipping school and speaking out against the powers that be. Wouldn't that make her a rebel too?

To understand Thunberg, we must be very careful to differentiate between what she thinks (consciously), what the public relations machine around her wants us to think and what she is archetypally (unconsciously). No doubt Thunberg thinks of herself as a rebel and that is true of her at the individual level. She did skip school against her parents' wishes and that was an act of rebellion within the Thunberg household. The problem is to what use this rebellion has been put and this is where the public relations machine comes into the picture. Thunberg's rise was not organic like a Peterson or a Trump. It was manufactured. Her social media posts about her school strike were immediately shared by high profile accounts. Within months, Thunberg was getting speaking gigs at environmental demonstrations around Europe and then came her famous speech at the UN. Thunberg went from unknown schoolgirl in Stockholm to giving speeches at the UN within four months. In 2019 she became Time's Person of the Year and was a given a string of other awards as long as your arm; all awards granted by the establishment. Remember that one of the properties of The Devouring Mother is she gives her children false praise. That is what has been happening with Thunberg. As the saying goes, it takes years to create an overnight success. Peterson's story shows that formula very clearly. Thunberg's does not. Thunberg might have been a rebel at the individual level but the people who have hoisted her to fame are the establishment. When you bear in mind that environmentalism these days is run out of the establishment, this makes perfect sense. As a young woman with Asperger's Syndrome, it seems very unlikely that Thunberg understands this.

To put it in the archetypal terms we have been using, Thunberg was embraced by The Devouring Mother. We might therefore expect her to be The Orphan in the relationship and given her age and social status this would be fitting. But this is where things get symbolically weird. Again, we must take care to differentiate between two different realms. There is what Thunberg is archetypally as an individual and there is what she has been portrayed as. In the latter case, she is The Orphan, a lone schoolgirl making a stand against the system. In the former, the evidence suggests she is The Devouring Mother i.e. The Caregiver in shadow form. Recall the properties of The Devouring Mother: she seeks martyrdom, she emotionally manipulates others, she aims to win control through guilt tripping. Thunberg ticks all the boxes. People in the mainstream media talk unironically about how Thunberg just wants to "save the world". That is a prime case of martyrdom. But this martyrdom itself is highly questionable. Although theoretically giving up her education for the greater good and therefore acting selflessly, Thunberg has in the process become a global phenomenon who has met world leaders, attended famous events and gone on adventures that no normal fifteen-year-old could dream of. Real martyrdom involves real sacrifice but, as Jung pointed out, The Devouring Mother is incapable of genuine sacrifice. There is nothing in the story of Thunberg that speaks of sacrifice; quite the opposite. What about emotional manipulation and guilt tripping? The official story goes that Thunberg attempted to convince her parents about the importance of climate change issues using graphs and numbers but when that didn't work she told them they were "stealing her future". If that isn't guilt tripping and emotional manipulation, I don't know what is. Moreover, it seems to have worked and Thunberg's parents agreed to give up flying and embrace other so-called environmental measures. Thunberg would later pull the same stunt in front of the world at the UN. These facts speak to a young girl who is a Caregiver archetype psychologically. But, like all teenagers, she is experimenting with her shadow. The teenage years are the developmental phase where we each face our shadow and the only real way to do that is to embody it first. Hence the difficulty of that phase of life. Most parents allow teenagers the leeway to do this knowing that it is a trial each of us must sort out for ourselves. This seems to be the approach that Thunberg's parents took too. That is why Thunberg has displayed all the attributes of a Devouring Mother. She is a teenager embodying the shadow side of The Caregiver archetype. The difference is that Thunberg was raised to global fame while manifesting her shadow. She has been rewarded for it by society. That is not healthy either for her or for society.

If Thunberg is The Caregiver/Devouring Mother at the personal level, how have the people who have hoisted her to fame wanted us to perceive her? We can find the answer in another snippet from Thunberg's biography. In May 2018, Thunberg submitted an entry to a climate change essay competition held by a Swedish Newspaper. In it she wrote "I want to feel safe". That should set off your synchronicity alarm bells because "I want to feel safe" is the very catchphrase of The Orphan. Recall that the primary desire of The Orphan is to achieve safety and their archetypal journey is to secure that safety for themselves. The shadow side of The Orphan is to play the victim and this is what is implied by the phrase "I want to feel safe": I do not feel safe and it is somebody else's job to make sure that I do. This is a request for special treatment due to feigned victimhood. Thunberg had learned to play the role of The Orphan as a guilt tripping device on her parents and was using the same tactic in her essay. The climate change movement had already begun invoking The Orphan archetype in its propaganda and now regularly makes use of schoolchildren as one of its primary political tactics. Thunberg's entry to the essay competition brought her to the attention of the people who were leaders of that movement and she was speaking the exact language they wanted to hear. No surprise then that she won the competition. According to the official story, after winning the essay contest, Thunberg was contacted by somebody from a climate NGO. We don't know what they talked about, but it was just three months later that she went on her school strike that was instantly amplified by climate NGOs and other establishment players. It went viral but the players who made it go viral were the establishment. The "I want to be safe" line, the image of a solitary young girl in front of the seat of power, combined with climate apocalypse fantasies are all traits of The Orphan. That is how the establishment wanted to portray Thunberg. Thunberg gave lip service to that perception but her behaviour and words reveal that she is a Caregiver/Devouring Mother. Let's take a look at some of the key phrases from Thunberg's famous speech at the UN.

Our house is on fire.

You are still not mature enough to tell it like it is.

...your betrayal...

We will never forgive you.

We will not let you get away with this.

And, of course, the most famous one –

How dare you!

These words are straight from the mouth of The Devouring Mother. As if that wasn't enough, the UN event gave us the iconic image of Thunberg scouring at Trump. A more perfect picture of The Devouring Mother vis-à-vis her rebellious children could not be found.

In Thunberg, we have a symbolic combination of The Devouring Mother and The Orphan. She comes from the upper class of Swedish society but is portrayed as just a lowly schoolgirl. She plays the victim while travelling the globe to meet celebrities. She speaks as a mother in the body of a child. She declares that she just wants to be "safe" while appearing in public with the most powerful people in the world, addressing huge crowds and generally doing things that almost no teenager would have the courage to do. If The Devouring Mother and The Orphan have together been ascendant in the West in recent decades, Thunberg is the ultimate symbol of them both. The Devouring Mother in the guise of The Orphan. But there is one final Jungian twist to the story. Thunberg as individual is an Orphan to The Devouring Mother at the societal level. All teenagers manifest their shadow. It is a core part of development. But with Thunberg we have the image of a young girl being encouraged to manifest her shadow for the benefit of others. This is precisely the enabling behaviour of The Devouring Mother; encouraging the child to manifest its shadow and not to individuate itself. That is what The Devouring Mother does to her children at the individual and the social level. It's part of the symbolic weirdness that, even though Thunberg is herself The Devouring Mother, in relation to the societal Devouring Mother she is really an Orphan; an acquiescent child. Thunberg is being denied the normal development that should take place in the teenage years. She has become reliant on The Devouring Mother (the establishment) for her fame. If and when that gets taken away, the results for her are likely to be very painful. Sadly this wilful and shameful disregard for the welfare of a young girl is all too common now in our culture and has been on full display throughout corona. The Devouring Mother only pretends to care about the interests of the young. Her actions speak very differently. In Thunberg we have a symbol of the *relationship* between Devouring Mother and Orphan. She is the combination of the two. She is both the mother and the child. Both the enabler and the enabled. The receiver of false praise and the giver of emotional manipulation and guilt tripping. Both the victim and the victimiser. Young in form, old in spirit. Unrestrained will to power masquerading as innocence. In Thunberg, modern politics approaches old fashioned myth. That is not a positive development. It speaks to a retreat from logic and pragmatism and, although we didn't know it at the time, foreshadowed the approach of the psychic epidemic that has been corona.

Climate change and the environmental movement had already become a weapon in the hands of The Devouring Mother prior to Thunberg but with her it reached new heights. Modern climate change propaganda is an apocalypse fantasy aimed at The Orphans. It represents the powerless and the victimhood mentality that is at the core of The Orphan's shadow. In this way, it was a precursor to corona. Did you notice how all the climate stuff came abruptly to an end as soon as corona kicked off? We effortlessly swapped from apocalypse fantasies about climate to apocalypse fantasies about respiratory viral disease.

The latter works better as a manipulation device for the obvious reason that a pandemic represents an immediate threat while even the most dire climate predictions are way off into the future. It was mostly this that enabled The Orphan archetype to "go viral". The end being sought was a psychological one. None of this is to say that there aren't real issues at play. There are. Respiratory viral disease is a real thing and so is climate change. But, as we have seen, the issues have been co-opted for political purposes and the politics has been not about the real issues but about psychological manipulation.

There is one final point to make about climate change and pandemics. They are both, to use a very useful distinction coined by John Michael Greer, predicaments, not problems. A problem has a solution. A predicament is something that simply must be worked through. Throughout history, humans treated every pandemic as if it was a predicament. Corona is the first time we have treated one as if it was a problem. It was this key change in The Plague Story that I identified in my first book on corona. We started telling ourselves the story that pandemics had solutions. But that story had no basis in reality. There has never been a respiratory pandemic that was ended with a vaccine. The story was also a myth and further represents the flight from reality that our society is suffering from. The same pattern can be seen with climate change. Climate change is a predicament, arguably the oldest predicament faced by mankind. Climate change has been with us ever since humans appeared on this earth. Somehow, we survived through the ice ages and the warming periods without any modern technology but now we are told that the future of the entire planet is our responsibility. Of course, the "problem" is so enormous that it is out of the hands of the average person to solve it. For that, we need "the experts". People can work through predicaments all by themselves. Experts solve problems. Of course, we've also made it through endless pandemics and endless variants of the respiratory viruses that we have co-evolved with. Sars-cov-2 is just another one of those. Colds and flus are predicaments at the individual level. In our culture, we teach children from a very young age how to handle a predicament. You go to bed, rest and wait for the worst to pass. The ones who love you will take care of you and give you extra attention and support and then you can get on with your life. *This too shall pass.* That was how we used to treat pandemics but now we appear set to ensure that they become endless problems. If you can convince someone that a predicament is a problem, you can sell them the solution and you can keep selling them the solution because predicaments never end. There will never not be climate change and there will never not be respiratory viruses. All this is just another way to phrase The Devouring Mother archetype. The Devouring Mother wants an endless relationship of co-dependence. That is exactly the type of relationship that happens when you are stuck buying a solution to a predicament. The end is always just around the corner. The "solution" is always arriving and never arrives. That is co-dependence. That is The Devouring Mother at work.

Chapter 5: The Archetypal Mask

There is one aspect of the symbolism of the corona event that is worth delving into in some detail and that is the mask. The wearing of a mask ostensibly to prevent the transmission of respiratory viral disease was unknown in western culture until 2020 (yes, there are the pictures from the Spanish flu to show that people in some places wore masks back then. The fact that nobody remembered them proves that they didn't exist in our cultural memory). In Asian cultures, it is considered polite to wear a mask if you are feeling sick in order to protect others but this was simply not a thing in the west. In fact, prior to 2020, you could go to work in a poorly ventilated office, hop into the sardine can of public transport or take an international airflight and cough and sneeze to your heart's content and nobody would have batted an eyelid. The imposition of masks was therefore a big deal in a strictly cultural sense but, by the time we'd got around to making masks mandatory, we'd also thrown out the rulebook on a whole host of other elements of our culture including the established public health strategy on dealing with a pandemic. I discussed in The Plague Story how masks became tied in with a kind faux-heroism at the start of corona. People who were supposedly trying to convince others to wear masks would reference some sportsperson or sports team who were wearing masks and say something like "if they can do it while playing elite sports, you can do it while going to the supermarket." I noted at the time that the tone of these calls was derogatory in nature. They didn't call for real heroism but simply to fall in line and do what you were told. Viewed through the lens of The Devouring Mother and Orphan, such calls are examples of the emotional manipulation engaged in by both archetypes. What's the big deal, we were told. It's just a little mask. But masks are a big deal. They are a big deal because they are a powerful symbol that resonates in the unconscious and, despite our culture's wilful ignorance of the darker parts of the psyche, the unconscious mind drives most behaviour and sets a tone for the world in which we live. The reason why so much of modern politics targets the subconscious is precisely because people are easily led that way as our culture does not educate them on the matter. We are supposed to be a scientific society but there is no scientific evidence that masks stop the spread of respiratory viruses. Numerous randomised control trials have shown no effect from mask wearing. That should have been a problem. It should also have been a problem when we wore the masks anyway and they clearly made no difference. But we kept wearing them. That is the practical, scientific side of the matter. The symbolic way that masks resonate in the unconscious is the more important side for our purposes as it ties in directly with the shadow archetypes which have taken over during corona. As we are about to see, the mask covering the mouth has a very clear denotation in the unconscious.

The approach we're going to take is one used by Jung himself. It involves analysing stories for archetypal content. Jung was particularly interested in myths and fairy tales as he believed that, like dreams, they referenced the collective unconscious in the most direct fashion. "The psyche contains all the images that have ever given rise to myths," Jung once wrote. Myths feature simplified characters and plot and one of the effects of this simplification is to strip away the rationalisations of the conscious mind and get down into what is essential at the depths of the psyche. The only kinds of masks I am aware of from ancient myth and fairy tale are the full face masks which are a near universal of human religious practice. As such, we can't go looking there for an understanding of the masks that people have been wearing during corona. There is, however, a related genre from modern times which feature masks and that is the superhero film. Superhero films are in many ways the modern equivalent to myths and fairy tales. They are often derived from comic books and have a strong bias towards imagery which is in line with the approach taken in myth. In fact, it's not unusual to see characters from myth in superhero films. As the Marvel franchise can attest, superhero stories are as popular today as were the myths and fairy tales of old and from this we can deduce that they resonate strongly with the unconscious. In the Jungian sense, they should be the perfect place to go looking for archetypes and, when we do so, it turns out that superhero films have something very interesting to tell us about the symbolism of masks.

As an exercise, picture in your mind a superhero; not any particular superhero, just a generic, run-of-the-mill, about-to-save-the-world kind of superhero. What is your superhero wearing? Chances are they are wearing a cape. The cape is the article of clothing most synonymous with superheroes, hence the facetious saying "not all heroes wear capes". A pair of spandex tights probably comes in a close second. There is also a very good chance your superhero is wearing a mask but it won't be the kind of mask people have been wearing during corona. It will be a mask that wraps around the superhero's eyes. Possibly the earliest example of this kind of masked superhero was Zorro who appeared in 1919. There have been countless others since then in comic books and film. The superhero mask that covers the eyes is derived from the masquerade mask. The purpose of the masquerade mask, and the masquerade ball more generally, was to allow the upper class of European society to hide their identity and thereby to escape the social constraints of their time and let their hair down for an evening. That's also the purpose of the superhero mask: to hide the hero's identity. When somebody has multiple identities, they are said to have an *alter ego* and this is another standard trope of superhero stories. The superhero steps out of their normal, humdrum existence and saves the world. The superhero's mask reinforces that trope. Just as the masquerade mask allows people to drop their normal personality and free themselves from social constrictions, so the superhero's mask allows them to tap into their deeper strengths and perform amazing feats while not being recognised by the authorities or the people they know. Clark Kent's glasses in Superman function in a similar way although it is the removal of the glasses that symbolises the alter ego and allows Kent to masquerade undetected as Superman.

Now let's try the same exercise with a supervillain. Try to picture a stereotypical supervillain in your mind. Chances are this will not be such an easy exercise. Supervillains tend to come in different shapes and sizes and don't fit an obvious pattern as much as superheroes. What supervillains have in common is an exaggeration of some part of their physical or non-physical characteristics. They might be way too big or way too small. They might have a huge head or a small head, huge eyes or small eyes. They might be super smart as in the evil genius or psychopathically lacking in empathy (also as in the evil genius). Put simply, they are abnormal in some way. Comic books and superhero films are not shy about exaggerating this abnormality for effect. For example, in Mad Max Beyond Thunderdome, George Miller created a doppelvillain featuring the very small (Master) sitting on the shoulders of the very large (Blaster). The creators of Teenage Mutant Ninja Turtles would later use the same idea with the villainous Krang being lugged around by a large humanoid creature. This exaggerated combination of elements that are out of balance, unnatural and hideous is the hallmark of the villain.

Supervillains also wear masks but there are crucial difference between the mask of the superhero and those of the supervillain. There are three primary types of supervillain mask. The first is the one which is necessary for their survival as the villain carried a permanent wound or injury. This is almost always a breathing apparatus and hence covers the mouth. Darth Vader is the prime example. Another example is Immortan Joe, the villain in Mad Max Fury Road who requires a complicated breathing apparatus to survive. A third example is the Bane character from the Batman franchise. In the story, Bane's mask releases the painkillers which he needs in order to overcome the pain from his injuries. In Vader, Immortan Joe and Bane we have the supervillain whose mask is a direct symbol of their compromised physical state. Such characters are often taking revenge on the world for the perceived injustice of their injury. It is worth noting that Vader is one of the proto-villains of modern western culture and he wears a mask. The breathing apparatus mask is one of the most frightful in the unconscious as it relates to the primal fear of suffocation.

The second type of supervillain mask is that which serves to induce fear directly, which is useful thing to do if you're a bad guy. These are almost always full face masks. The Jason character from the Friday the 13th franchise is perhaps the perfect exemplar of this. The balaclava is another example. These masks are common in the horror genre because they dehumanise the character and turn a human into nothing more than a force of nature which cannot be reasoned with. The mask worn in the movie Scream is another prime example. Darth Vader's mask also fits in this category. George Lucas based it on the old samurai masks in Japan which were meant to instill fear into an opponent (just like we have had fear instilled into us during corona by being surrounded by people wearing masks). On this score, it is noteworthy that when Tom Cruise played a samurai (kind of) in the movie The Last Samurai he went without the face mask in the final scene as the other samurai rode into battle fully masked; further evidence that the good guys' and the bad guys' masks are mutually exclusive.

The third kind of mask is the mask which covers the villain's mouth only. An example of this is the ninja mask, although this has more to do with western cultural representations of ninjas than historical reality. There is no evidence that the ninjas in Japan wore masks so this seems to have been something added by western culture, which is a revealing fact by itself. Examples of this kind of mask is the one worn by the Shredder character in Teenage Mutant Ninja Turtles. Another is The Winter Soldier from the Captain America franchise whose black mouth-covering mask is an exact replica of the mask that would become synonymous with the year 2020. It's notable that the character in the film is brainwashed by Hydra (another mythological reference) and the brainwashing breaks down when his mask is removed. A subtype of the mouth-covering mask is the muzzle. Max is made to wear one of these in the movie Mad Max Fury Road and his first desire on regaining his freedom is to remove it. Similarly, in The Silence of the Lambs, Anthony Hopkins wore the muzzle that became the image that was synonymous with the movie.

To some extent, these categorisations are arbitrary and there is significant symbolic overlap. Shredder's mask, for example, is clearly meant to instil fear in his opponent while Bane and Immortan Joe's masks fit into all three categories. The common properties to all supervillain masks are that they are dehumanising, frightening, hide the character's true intent, often alter their voice, keep them from speaking (truth) and remove the expressiveness of the human face. None of these properties is true of the superhero's mask. The main exception to this is the hero who wears a full face mask. Such characters fall into two main types. Firstly, there are the anti-heroes such as V in *V for Vendetta*. By definition, these are heroes who have something wrong with them. They are often vigilantes and, though they act for good, they carry a fatal flaw within. In this way, they are like a villain, though they act for good. Secondly, there are shapeshifter characters such as Spiderman, Iron Man or The Mask. In these cases, the mask (whether alone or as part of a larger outfit) symbolises a complete transformation. The mask confers special powers on the character and they shapeshift out of their ordinary existence and into something else. This is just an extension of the alter ego trope and thus the full face mask is a variation on the eye mask and represents more strongly the fact that the hero has left their normal life and personality behind. These exceptions prove the rule. Masks covering the mouth in particular, and the face in general, are exclusively the domain of bad guys. It's not the case that all supervillains wear masks over their mouths but it is the case that all characters in superhero stories who wear masks over their mouths are villains. I couldn't find a single example where a hero character had their mouth covered. On this subject, our culture (reflecting the unconscious mind) is quite unanimous: wearing a mask over your mouth signals there is something wrong with you; something to be feared.

With this in mind, one would have expected a lot of unwillingness to wear masks during the corona event and this was indeed the case among certain segments of the population. In the northern hemisphere autumn of 2020, Rory Sutherland, an advertising guru who writes entertainingly in The Spectator and other publications, tried to solve the problem of how to sell masks to a reluctant public. Apparently, it was men who were most reluctant, so Sutherland came up with the idea of re-branding the mask as something exciting. The way to do this was to wear a cool hat and perhaps a bandana over your mouth instead of a mask. That way you could look like a bad mofo out for a bit of trouble rather than somebody who was just conforming to social pressure. I'm not sure whether Sutherland knew it, but the character he was describing, the "international man of mystery", was The Shadow. The Shadow first appeared in comic book form back in the 1930s wearing a fedora hat and a scarf wrapped around his face covering his mouth and chin. The character was an anti-hero vigilante who was versed in the dark arts. Later, in the radio series where he was voiced by Orson Welles, he would catch the bad guys by virtue of the fact that he was invisible. Sutherland's attempt at rebranding the corona mask to the kind worn by The Shadow was a clever piece of marketing that makes sense within the archetypal analysis of this chapter. It was an attempt to the change the mask from the kind that covers the mouth and symbolises illness to the kind The Shadow wore which symbolises covertness. Sutherland wanted to swap the stigma of the villain for the ambivalence and edginess of the anti-hero. The international man of mystery needs to go around undetected and the scarf covering the mouth achieves that in the same way that the ninja mask does (although, to reiterate, this kind of mask seems to have been invented by western interpretations of the ninja and is not based on historical fact). On the scale of villainy, the scarf or bandana over the mouth is less villainous than any of the other options including the faux-surgical masks people have been wearing during corona. It was a credible effort from Sutherland. But it's still the case that, within the broader archetypal analysis of this book, he was trying to get people, men in particular, to acquiesce to the mask idea. He was doing so in the exact same way that others were: appealing to hero-ism except that, unlike the derogatory nature of the other calls, Suther-land was inviting you to be an anti-hero. The problem is that this is still a symbolic inversion of unconscious reality. Whether on the face of a vil-lain or an anti-hero, the mask symbolises there is something wrong with you. It can never be the mask of the true hero. To submit to the mask is to acknowledge that there is something wrong.

In the history of superhero stories, the anti-hero character evolved partly due to the lack of psychological sophistication in the superhero. The invocation of The Shadow is very fitting in this respect because *The Shadow knows what evil lurks in the hearts of men*. That was the catch-phrase from the radio version of the comic and it nicely summarises the anti-hero. The difference between the anti-hero and the full-blown vil-lain is that the former knows the difference between good and evil and struggles to do good. The latter does not. The anti-hero fights against their shadow while the villain embodies it. In a well-told hero's journey, the psychological battle is as important as fighting an external enemy. I'm not sure if George Lucas had read Jung, but his use of "the dark side" in the Star Wars movies is very accurate on this score. The hero is tempted to go to the dark side (of their archetype) and their psycho-logical struggle is to resist that urge. The difference between the good guys and the bad guys, between the superheros and the supervillains, is that the latter have gone to the dark side. Traditionally, the super-hero was rather ignorant of the dark side and the supervillain was igno-rant of the good side. That was where anti-heroes like The Shadow or V came along. They know the power of the shadow from direct experi-ence. They have gone to the dark side and returned, although they carry some permanent scarring from the experience. One way to think about this is that the anti-hero is in their shadow striving for good while the hero is in the good striving not to fall into the shadow. To the extent that the anti-hero wears a mask, it is to symbolise that they too are in the shadow.

What all this amounts to is that the mask symbolises the shadow di-rectly. Characters wearing the mask, in particular the mask that covers the mouth, are in their shadow. This is true for both villains and anti-heroes. We can deduce that this is how they are perceived by the unconscious mind. If that's the case, then forcing the population to wear masks would also be forcing them to be in their shadow and that is exactly what is predicted by our archetypal analysis. Both The Devouring Mother and The Orphan are in their shadow. To the extent that these archetypes took over during corona, the mask is symbolically concordant. Some people have said that we have been sick until proven healthy during corona and the masks are the symbolic representation of that fact. Our politicians were telling us as much. In the Australian winter of 2021, with Sydney experiencing a lockdown that seemed like it would never end, the Premier of NSW told the public at a press conference that they should assume every stranger on the street had corona. This is what the masks were really for. They were a subconscious symbol to the population that their fellow citizens were diseased. They were also a symbol that we were in a psychic epidemic, an archetypal takeover by the shadow forms of The Devouring Mother and The Orphan. The wearing of masks during corona makes sense not just as a general marker of the shadow but within the specific forms of these two archetypes. The sick until proven healthy notion corresponds to The Devouring Mother in her Munchausen by Proxy form where the mother feigns illness in her otherwise healthy child. During corona, it didn't matter that you had no symptoms of illness. It didn't matter that the overwhelming majority of the population experienced the virus as nothing more than a flu. It didn't matter that you'd already had the virus or the vaccine. You were required to wear the mask and symbolically feign illness for The Devouring Mother. In being required to wear the mask, we all became acquiescent children in the game of Munchausen by Proxy. The masks also fit within the archetype of The Orphan whose primary mission is to regain "safety". The Orphans demanded others wear the mask to keep them safe, a statement which has no scientific basis as masks don't work to prevent the transmission of viruses. It only ever existed as a psychological demand. The belief that justifies the masks at a quasi-scientific level is what I call the naïve germ theory of disease which states that we humans are just pure, empty vessels waiting for the virus to come and infect us. This is completely untrue of what we now know about the human body and its microbiological interactions with the environment, but the belief fits perfectly with the psychology of The Orphan. The Orphan has an immune system like everyone else. They are not defenceless and we now know they were never defenceless against the so-called "new" virus as cross immunity to sars-cov-2 seems to have been present from day one. But feigned powerlessness is one of The Orphan's primary shadow traits. The mask over the mouth provided only the illusion of physical protection but that was not the important part. The important part was the symbolism in the unconscious; a tacit admission of being in the shadow.

We have noted already that the acquiescent children divide the world up into the *good people* and the *bad people*. The masks became the prime symbol of that division. To have been a *good person* during corona was to wear the mask while those who refrained were at best inconsiderate, lacking in compassion or whatever other guilt tripping label came to mind. Of course, this so-called compassion did not extend to people who could not wear masks for medical reasons let alone psychological ones. This presents a seeming paradox because, as we have seen, the mask very clearly represents the shadow, illness and wrongness in the collective unconscious. Why would the *good people* want to symbolise themselves as the shadow, the bad guys? The paradox is resolved once we introduce the Munchausen by Proxy concept. Within the Munchausen by Proxy frame, being a *good child* is synonymous with either being sick or feigning sickness. When applied to corona, the desire to wear a mask is the desire to please the mother by feigning sickness. This corresponds to real world cases of Munchausen by Proxy. Psychiatrists have noted that the child can learn to desire the attention they get from The Devouring Mother when pretending to be sick. That is what the mother wants and what the child learns to want. The masks indulge the shadow side of The Orphan who desires special treatment even if that treatment is bad for them. Orphans love to play the victim and to victimise others through their victimhood. Mandatory masks do exactly that. During corona, we dressed the citizens of society like hospital patients. We made everybody pretend to be the victim and pretend to be powerless. We did it all in the name protecting others. Archetypally, we all became Orphans during corona: powerless, needing to protected, needing to be saved. That was the line at the start when we apparently didn't know enough about the virus and had to play it safe. Ironically, it wasn't until the middle of 2021 that masks became mandatory in most places and by that point we knew what the virus was. The data was then clear that the virus was dangerous to the elderly and immuno-compromised. The masks were unnecessary. We had changed from a pragmatic public health response to an archetypal takeover. The Plague Story had been invoked and we now needed to sit tight and wait to be rescued by the vaccines. Mandatory masks made sense at the unconscious level as a way to keep the population compliant until the vaccines were available. Some people refer to this kind of thing as a psy-op and the label is quite fitting. Whatever the actual health issues at play, corona has mostly been a psychic epidemic. The masks denote that very clearly. They made no sense scientifically but a lot of sense within our archetypal analysis of the unconscious. Some public health bureaucrats have already informed us that we will be wearing the masks for years to come even though the vaccine will be fully available. That may well happen. To the extent that it does happen, it won't have much to do with public health but it will be a very clear symbol that The Devouring Mother is still in the ascendant.

Chapter 6: Conclusion

This confrontation [with the shadow] is the first test of courage on the inner way, a test sufficient to frighten off most people, for the meeting with ourselves belongs to the more unpleasant things that can be avoided so long as we can project everything negative into the environment.

Carl Jung, The Archetypes and the Collective Unconscious

In one of the most scintillating passages from his Red Book, Jung describes in an extended metaphor the process of individuating. It's full of violent images: starving, strangling, smashing. "I will break your bones until there is no longer a trace of hardness there." He is talking to his "I". What Jung realised and spent much of his career investigating was that the "I" was just the tip of the iceberg; the jockey atop the horse; capable of some form of control but not the source of power. As any modern marketer, public relations expert or propagandist knows, the power comes from the emotions and the unconscious but it's very easy for the little "I" to get too big for its boots and start to think that it really is running the show. The unindividuated psyche projects its shadow through the "I". It maps its insecurities, fears and darker desires directly onto objects in the external world, including and especially other people. What makes the whole dynamic so difficult to deal with on a practical level is that the person usually has no idea they are doing it. How do you make somebody see something they aren't willing to see especially when the act of seeing is not going to be a pleasant experience? Jung talks of deliberately subjugating the "I" but in real life this happens mostly by chance. Things have to go "wrong". We must have our ego's bones broken through the vicissitudes of fate and be forced to undertake the journey to the depths. There's a seemingly throwaway lyric from one of my favourite rock musicians, Brant Bjork – "the losers are the chosen few". He's right. The losers are the chosen few who are invited to face the shadow and individuate. Most do not. Ask any lawyer who will be honest with you and they'll tell you that half their cases are just people projecting the shadow. Whether in business, in marriage or in other interpersonal relationships, we share the blame when things go wrong. It takes two to tango as the saying goes. The lawyer earns their fee by pretending that their client is perfectly innocent and the other party perfectly guilty; good guys vs bad guys like in a cheesy Hollywood action movie from the 80s. In reality, lawyers are getting paid so their client does not have to face the fact that they are just as much at fault as the other person. The loser in the fight can then blame the lawyer or the justice system or society instead of facing their shadow. Jung's metaphor of broken bones is correct. Individuating is hard. Most people will do anything to avoid it.

Doctors in modern society often fulfil a very similar psychological function to lawyers. I once had a fascinating conversation with a doctor who had emigrated from India to Australia. I asked her what differences she noticed between the two countries and she said "in India, my patients were actually sick." She estimated about half of her patients had nothing physically wrong with them. It was all "in their head". Viral disease is a relationship between us and the virus where our general health is a big factor in determining how sick we will get from an infection. Our society has completely ignored this relationship and pretended the virus was solely responsible much like a lawyer pretends their client is perfectly innocent and the other party completely guilty. Modern medicine treats many lifestyle conditions like high blood pressure with medicines rather than addressing the underlying cause. That's a profitable business model but it ends up doing more harm than good. This blindness to the relational nature of disease is therefore another example of projecting the shadow. Integrating one's psyche is exactly the act of recognising the relationships that exist within it, including the shadow. It's about coming to terms with the darker elements of one's mind. It's about taking responsibility for it in the same way one should take responsibility for one's health. This lack of responsibility has manifested in multiple ways during corona but perhaps not more ironically than in the offers of alcohol, donuts, burgers and other kinds of junk food as incentives for getting the vaccine all while the corona statistics show a clear and strong correlation between lifestyle disease and serious illness from corona. Of course, corona correlates most strongly with the ultimate lifestyle disease: old age. As yet, we have no medical intervention to deal with that. Life will kill ya, sang Warren Zevon and a more concise summary of the situation has not been uttered. Whatever the underlying health issue posed by corona, it has been completely distorted by the politics and psychology at play (almost all of modern politics is really about psychology). This psychology blew up in what I originally called a mass hysteria or what Jung called a mass movement. In The Plague Story, I tried to identify the individual factors which led to this happening as if they were all small causes that combined in some unique way to create the hysteria. It was a bottom-up approach. In this book, I have taken a top-down approach. The pattern which connects all these seemingly disparate factors are the archetypes of The Devouring Mother, The Orphan in shadow form and the rebellious children. The meta-pattern which sits on top is the psychic epidemic. Some people have likened corona to Nazi Germany and this is correct in the sense that both are psychic epidemics; archetypal takeovers of society.

*If we cannot deny the archetypes or otherwise neutralize them,
we are confronted, at every new stage in the differentiation of
consciousness to which civilisation attains, with the task of finding a new interpretation appropriate to this stage, in order to
connect the life of the past that still exists in us with the life of
the present, which threatens to slip away from it. If this link-up
does not take place, a kind of rootless consciousness comes into
being no longer oriented to the past, a consciousness which suc-
cumbs helplessly to all manner of suggestions and, in practice, is
susceptible to psychic epidemics.*

We become susceptible to psychic epidemics when we lack the interpretation which links the current stage of society back to the past.
The desire for rootedness, for a connection back to history, brings us
right back to Jordan Peterson and the rebellious children. Peterson's lectures on the bible stories and other myths offered that cultural link to
the past that the rebellious children seek. Even Trump's *Make America
Great Again* is a call to re-establish a link to the past. This link is no tri-
fling matter. It is a necessary element of psychic health without which
we are open to suggestion and susceptible to psychic epidemics such as
corona. Of course, there are other forces in society which promote the
opposite; a radical revision or even rejection of the past with the seeming aim to break free from it. We saw this very explicitly in the summer
of 2020 in the USA with the tearing down of statues and the desecra-
tion of monuments across the country. It is implied in concepts of The
Great Reset and the 4th Industrial Revolution. It is the idea that sits at
the heart of the climate change propaganda. There is a logic to it within
the story that gets told there. The past represents fossil fuel pollution
and that is what we must get rid of. Ergo, we must break with the past.
This "break" with the past in practice amounts to nothing more than
projecting the shadow. We take all the elements we don't like about current society and project the blame for them into the past thereby absolv-
ing ourselves from responsibility. A proper way to individuate would be

to come to terms with those things and to incorporate them into our current worldview. It is therefore no surprise that the people who follow that way of thinking have been the most susceptible to the psychic epidemic of corona as they are most likely to explicitly reject a connection with the past. We have used the archetype of The Orphan in this book to explain corona. That archetype is exactly the one which suffers from rootlessness. The break with one's own parents is the most direct separation from history at the personal level. It's noteworthy that this separation from the parents is quite literally true in the modern west where the divorce rate in the last fifty or so years has increased substantially meaning that many more people have grown up in one parent households. But the pattern holds at the societal level too. Greta Thunberg represents the break from the parents both at the household level and at the societal. "How dare you" is the projection of the shadow onto the parents. Thunberg's words work at the personal level and also the sociocultural.

This dynamic also demonstrates the usual tension between progressivism (liberalism) and conservatism only it has been ratcheted up to new levels in recent times. Another quote from Jung is pertinent on this front:

> But our progressiveness, though it may result in a great many delightful wish-fulfilments, piles up an equally gigantic Promethean debt which has to be paid off from time to time in the form of hideous catastrophes.

Jung almost certainly had the world wars in mind when writing this. The new "improvements" in weaponary did unleash hideous catastrophes most notably on the western front and at Hiroshima and Nagasaki. The corona event has also been made possible by technological innovations of which the PCR is the primary one. Corona is the first pandemic in history where the PCR test was used on a mass scale. The definition of a "case" as a single positive test had never been used before. It was trialled in the swine flu false alarm of 2009 but it wasn't until corona that the infrastructure was in place and the global laboratory network was able to spring into action in a coordinated fashion. Throughout corona, the average person has understood "case" in the old-fashioned sense of the word to mean a person who is really sick. But the case definition no longer means that. It just means a positive result on the PCR. Of course, the test results, the "cases" were able to be shared around the world instantaneously via another technological innovation: the internet. Alongside the further innovation of social media, the "case" numbers and graphs and other statistics spread along with emotional narratives given by people who clearly didn't understand the underlying meaning. Even a simple word like "case" needs to be understood technically to be able to put it into context. But context was missing. Corona also saw the introduction of other new meanings for words. The word "vaccine" now includes gene therapy technology. "Herd immunity" no longer includes natural immunity but only the "immunity" achieved through "vaccination". "Pandemic" now means any disease that spreads over a geographical area irrespective of how many people die. "Diseased" no long means that you have tangible symptoms but that you return a positive test result. All these words need inverted commas to remind us to check our understanding. What has been lacking throughout corona was "interpretation"; the story that would link these changes back to past meanings and allow the public to put the new words and new technology in proper context. The invalid invocation of The Plague Story occurred because these new meanings were not understood in the general culture.

Of course, the story itself was new and without historical foundation. As I noted in The Plague Story, the new ending to the story of pandemic, the one where the experts save the day, has no basis in history. There never has been a plague where a cure was found that ended the matter. The one time we tried something similar – the swine flu false alarm of 1976 – it was a complete failure. The modern plague story has only ever worked in Hollywood movies. What does it say about our society that we decided to pursue such an outcome? Are we no longer able to tell the difference between fact and fiction; between historical reality and Hollywood movies? At time of writing (mid-2021), it is becoming clear that the vaccines do not "work" in the sense that they do not prevent infection. Because of that, they do not stop the virus from mutating and, because RNA viruses mutate incredibly quickly, this means the virus will simply mutate around whatever the latest vaccine is. Even by the new definition of "herd immunity", the new "vaccine" cannot do what was implied by the new Plague Story. Of course, experts in the field already knew that. They just weren't the ones who made it onto the nightly news or into the halls of power. In this way, corona represents a very clear case study of exactly what Jung was talking about. In the absence of the links back to the past that would have enabled the public to make sense of what was happening, we pursued a story that was make believe. As the story failed to come true, this only served to heighten the hysteria.

With corona, we were ripe for a psychic epidemic precisely because we lack an interpretation of modern society that links us back to the past. The Devouring Mother and The Orphan, the two archetypes that have been ascendant in recent decades, are the ones who deliberately problematise such an interpretation. For them, the past is scorched earth. We must march onwards to a bright new future (although I challenge whether any normal person would find anything *bright* about The Great Reset or the Fourth Industrial Revolution). What differentiates The Devouring Mother's archetypal takeover from Wotan's in Nazi Germany is the speed with which it occurred; slowly, oh so slowly. The Devouring Mother tells her children that individuation is not necessary in order to continue the co-dependence relationship. Just like the poison apple offered by the evil Queen to Snow White, it looks appealing but hides a malicious intent. Acquiescing to The Devouring Mother is a giving in that happens over months and years one slightly poisoned apple at a time. Human nature being what it is, people inevitably come up with reasons why the slightly poisoned apple isn't that bad. It's food, after all, and you can barely even taste the poison after a while. Some people get around it by making up delusional dreams about the future.

Just one more bullshit job and then you'll have enough money to retire early. Some people get around it by making up apocalypse fantasies such as those provided by the modern climate change narrative. Such an intricate webs of lies and self-deceptions starts to cause its own problems. Freud and Jung in their psychiatric work often had to break through the surface level manifestations before they could get down to what was really driving the complexes displayed by their patients. The longer one stays under the roof of The Devouring Mother, the more complexes one builds up, the more difficult it becomes to escape and the more work is required to deal with the lies and cover ups protecting you from facing your shadow. But once the child has broken free of the gaslighting and the emotional manipulation, change is irreversible. The child has seen the poison apple for what it is.

The dynamic of The Devouring Mother is one of stifling psychological change. The archetypal analysis laid out in this book implies which changes that must happen to incorporate the shadow. The Devouring Mother, as the shadow of The Caregiver archetype, must learn compassion that is not grounded in selfishness. She must allow others and herself room to grow without trying to smother everything in order to hold onto an illusory control. The Orphan must learn to be comfortable with itself, to take responsibility for itself and to achieve things by itself. The rebellious children need to find the freedom to individuate in whatever way is right for them. If we take these archetypal patterns and map them onto society at large, what do we get? Here are just a few ideas.

- A winding back of consumerism and a return to real work. This would turn people from passive consumers into creators of actual wealth again. It would give people an autonomous economic identity that is so important no matter what kind of society you live in.
- A winding back of globalisation and return to local community. There must be a separation to allow room for people and nations to grow in whatever way is best rather than be stifled by some centralised power that doesn't have individual needs at heart. This

may also take the form of a separation within nations into smaller cultural groups again as people seek others who share their values. We're already seeing that happen politically and not just in narrative terms. Brexit was exactly this kind of separation. In the US, corona has led to a genuine difference in political philosophy with states such as Florida and Texas going their own way in direct contradiction to the federal government. The EU has managed to re-open internal borders but only by way of implementing yet more regulations and taxes. Want to cross a border in Europe now? You'll have to pay in the form of either a vaccine or a negative test result. One of the cornerstones of the neoliberal ideology was the free movement of people. Now we have the conditional movement of people and the early signs are that the "vaccine" is not going to reverse that trend. That will only lead to re-localisation.

- This is all against the backdrop of the US empire's power waning. Trump was the harbinger of that. America will no longer be the policeman of the world, he said. The post war order, set up largely in opposition to the madness unleashed by Wotan, has now itself descended into its shadow. The process ahead is the working out of what comes next.

All of this is against the prime requirement implied by Jung's quote from above. We need a new interpretation that links back to the past and enables us to make sense of how we got to where we are. That requirement is going to occur against a backdrop of political division. The grand narratives of the last several decades look to be gone and the needed interpretations are going to have to come from sources other than the official channels. For that reason, they are going to be more local, more niche, but also more personal and individualised. Of course, these interpretations are likely to meet significant resistance. The same psychic forces present during corona which have been building for decades are not simply going to slip away. In fact, they may become even more dominant in the years to come. The road ahead is likely to be neither easy nor short. It took two world wars to incorporate the shadow represented by Wotan and it may now take a similar amount of time to incorporate The Devouring Mother.

Appendix A: The Land of the Unfree and the Home of the Safe

I noted in The Plague Story that the story of pandemic is one of the oldest known to man and is a universal of human experience that cuts across cultures. The same is true of The Devouring Mother archetype as it relates to the mother-child relationship that is a human universal. Whereas in the years leading up to WW2 it was clear that something unique was happening in Germany, The Devouring Mother's reach has transcended national boundaries. However, it's also true that corona has played out very differently in different countries. Sweden was the most notable dissenting country in the west with Tanzania one of the more interesting outside the west, not least because their former president was a chemist by profession and was able to demonstrate the weakness of the PCR test, a weakness that had already been explained by the inventor of the technology, Kary Mullis, but to which western leaders and bureaucrats seemed completely oblivious. Here I'm going to focus on a country at the other end of the spectrum, one where the archetypal takeover has been most pronounced. It just happens to be the country where I live: Australia. By mid-2021, things had gotten so bad in Australia that we even came to the attention of certain sections of the US mainstream media. But, even before that, I had been in conversations online with individual Americans who simply couldn't believe what they were seeing in Australia. Our response to corona, initially successful and the "envy of the world", slowly and surely devolved into an authoritarian nightmare. The prosperous, freedom-loving, easy-going Australia that the world thought it knew had disappeared. In this chapter, I'll try to explain why in Jungian terms. I have decided to put this in the appendix rather than the main body of the text as it opens up a field of study that could itself require a book to explore; namely, a cross cultural analysis of the corona event. I invite the reader to compare the description below to the nation where they live and tease out the differences for themselves.

How to describe the madness of corona in Australia? I could easily blurt out pages and pages describing the army checkpoints, the soldiers on the streets of our major cities, the police brutality, the endless cycle of lockdowns, the heartlessness and stupidity of the public health bureaucrats, the innumerable blunders from the government, the lack of accountability and (real) leadership, the absurd fear-mongering from politicians and media and, perhaps most strikingly, the complete inability to raise a single dissenting voice that mattered to talk about it. All those things got worse, not better, as corona progressed. Back in March 2020, the Prime Minister told Australians the truth: everybody would get the virus but only the elderly and immuno-compromised were at risk. That was still true by mid-2021 but instead of that calm, rational and sensible approach, we had soldiers on the streets of Sydney, police helicopters looking out for lockdown heretics and all kinds of other craziness. Viewed from elsewhere in the world, this looked like what it was: absurd overreaction. Inside the country, we had been like frogs in the boiling water not realising how extreme things had got, which is a strange fact in itself in these times of global communication. Partly, this was because we couldn't raise a single dissenting voice that mattered in our public debate to actually talk about what was happening. The only critical voices we did raise focused on the politics, but that was the easy road to take. It's pleasant to think that the only thing we needed were better politicians to guide us out of the mess. But the politicians, especially in democracies, can only do what the public wants and the actions of the politicians in Australia had majority support. That reveals something about Australian culture and society. Or does it? How do we separate the Australian response from every other country? What do we attribute to fate and what to "character"?

The analytical problems to answer this question are several. Firstly, there is the fact that many countries around the world imposed draconian measures during corona. Australia was not alone there. Was the difference just a matter of degree or does it point to something deeper? Australia undoubtedly went further than other countries in many respects. We were unique, as far as I know, in not allowing citizens to leave without permission of government; a measure that was then extended to include citizens who had returned to Australia temporarily but who resided overseas. That's extreme but was it meaningfully different from restrictions imposed elsewhere? Unlike other countries, Australia was defending a "covid zero" position and it is this fact which constitutes the second analytical problem in comparing Australia to other countries. Once the borders were closed in early 2020, "cases" dropped like a rock. Unlike any other country in the world except New Zealand, Australia was presented with the opportunity of "eliminating the virus". Naturally, we took it. We then proceeded to tell ourselves that it wasn't blind luck but good management. More than that, we told ourselves it was because Australians cared about each other more than other countries, especially the US where everything is just "about money". If there's one pattern that's repeated in Australia throughout corona it's – *pride goeth before a fall*. No sooner had we finished patting ourselves on the back than the cracks started to show in the strategy courtesy of a never-ending procession of lockdowns. Melbourne was the first domino to fall in the winter of 2020. At time of writing, Melbourne is in lockdown number six while Sydney is in a lockdown that looks set to last longer than our epic three and-a-half-month effort last year. This all happened because, although borders were "closed", Australia still had to allow its citizens to return home and we still had to let Hollywood movie stars and other notables into the country because, in the words of the Queensland Chief Health Officer, they brought millions of dollars with them (yes, she actually said that with a straight face at a press conference). A quarantine program was set up but inevitably "cases" leaked out and outbreaks occurred. We didn't admit the obvious fact that this was a problem with the strategy of having quarantine facilities in heavily populated areas. Even purpose-built laboratories full of trained staff often fail to stop viruses getting out. Just ask the people in Wuhan. In Australia, we turned hotels in the major cities into quarantine facilities and populated them with barely trained staff. It's not like Australia has a shortage of land far away from population centres. It's not like we couldn't afford to build new facilities. The cost of our lockdowns counts in the trillions of dollars. It would have been cheaper to build a quarantine version of Dubai out in the desert. How long do viruses stay viable with the harsh Australian sun beating down on parched earth? Not long I would have thought. We'll never know because the Australian government couldn't organise it.

So, the lockdowns began. The first major one was here in Melbourne and, rather than admit a fault in the strategy and find a better way to do it, we found a way to pin the blame on the incompetent state government. No doubt the government was incompetent, most governments are. But we pretended that the state government in New South Wales knew what they were doing. They were the "gold standard" and, as long as everybody else copied them, the strategy would work. That charade lasted all the way into mid-2021 when New South Wales let an outbreak occur which led to a months-long lockdown which famously saw soldiers deployed on the streets of Sydney (hey, we had soldiers on the streets of Melbourne before it was cool). The cause of that lockdown was identical to the one in Melbourne a year earlier. History was repeating but we were not learning. Rather than try and discuss the matter objectively, the hysteria levels were raised higher than they had been at any time throughout corona. Politicians in all states embarked on a shameful program of fear mongering. It had nothing to do with health and everything to do with the fact they had been caught with their pants down. Having been happy to take the credit when times were good, they ramped up the hysteria when things went wrong. In the meantime, the federal government had failed to secure the vaccines that were supposed to end the whole thing. As a result, much of Australia spent essentially the whole flu season of 2021 in lockdown.

One of the earliest cultural critiques of Australia was a book called The Lucky Country by Donald Horne. To paraphrase the main message of the book: Australia is a lucky country run by second-rate people who share its luck. Corona couldn't bear that out more clearly. Although I obviously disagree with the strategy taken by western countries in relation to corona, there's no doubt that both the UK and the US were able to carry out that strategy properly. Australia was not. We fell backwards into a zero-covid strategy then proceeded to execute it with all the adroitness of a drunk wombat staggering through a nest of angry bull ants. Can we be held accountable for that? Does it reveal something about Australian society? Or is it unfair to blame politicians for an outcome they probably never believed possible and certainly would never have planned for? Would any other country have behaved differently if they had also stumbled into a situation where they got to "zero" and then had to defend that position?

A third analytical problem is one that is inherent in all exploration of Australian culture. It was noted by one of our earliest modern cultural critics, Robin Boyd: how to differentiate Australian culture from "international western culture". Australia became a nation on 1 January 1901 but the split from Britain was hardly clean. Britain still represented Australia in foreign affairs until the end of WW1. Australia placed armed forces at the disposal of Britain in both world wars. Radio and television news announcers still spoke with British accents until well after the middle of the 20th century. Politically, the main turning point came when Britain refused to defend Singapore in WW2 and left Australia to fend for itself against the Japanese. We turned to the US for help at which point we swapped from being part of the British empire to being part of the US empire. Australia had been dominated by British culture prior to the wars and then became dominated by US culture after. Wherever "Australian culture" has been in the short history of this country, it has had to be found beneath these dominant cultures. In the British era, that culture was found in the bush. The Man from Snowy River or Ned Kelly still hold a place in the nation's heart for that reason. It wasn't really until the 1970s that a distinctly Australian urban culture started to show through in television, movies, literature and music but it has always been dominated by US influence. Then came globalisation and multiculturalism to make things even more opaque.

I first encountered this problem in a practical sense when an Indian colleague flew to Melbourne for a project we were working on. On his first day we took him for lunch at a ramen noodle bar. Then, at the end of the week we went to a Chinese restaurant. Sometime in the middle of his second week, he came over and asked me for a recommendation for lunch – "where can I find Australian food?" he asked. That seemingly simple question proved very difficult to answer. What is Australian food exactly? I could have pointed him to Indian, Chinese, Japanese, Italian, there was even a Mongolian restaurant nearby. But there was no obviously "Australian" restaurant. The same is true of Australian culture in general. It's there but it's hidden away. Boyd called Australian culture a veneer on international western culture. That's one way to think about it. Another is that it is hiding beneath international western culture. Just like my colleague looking for "Australian" food, you have to ask for directions on how to find it.

What is partly at stake in these analytical issues is the age old question of free will versus determinism. The deterministic way to look at it is that, through the vicissitudes of fate, Australia accidentally ended up with no covid and then had to defend that position because, well, who wouldn't? According to this way of thinking, even the US would have had an endless procession of lockdowns, army checkpoints, police brutality and all the other things we have seen here in Australia if they were defending a covid-zero position. I'm quite certain that this is not true and in this chapter I hope to explain why by reference back to the archetypes we have seen in this book. The question can be framed this way: if corona is an archetypal takeover, why was Australia so much more affected than the US in particular and other western nations in general? When the archetypes take over, free will as determined by the ego (the conscious mind) disappears because the ego itself has been over-whelmed. The ego will still find "logical" and "rational" explanations for what is happening but these explanations are just projections from the unconscious. Thus, Australians have found explanations for why we ended up where we did e.g. we care more about each other than other countries, it's part of our egalitarian spirit etc. That explanation is not just a projection, it's a projection specific to the archetype which con-stitutes the Australian psyche which is, synchronistically, the one we have already seen in this book: The Orphan. The Devouring Mother took charge and Australia became an authoritarian nightmare. Why? The reason lies in the collective psychology of the country. What hap-pened in Australia during corona could never have happened in the US. Corona laid bare the real cultural-psychological differences that exist be-tween the two countries. If, as Robin Boyd pointed out, Australian cul-ture normally hides beneath US influence, corona brought it out from hiding. What has been revealed?

The short answer is that Australia is The Orphan and the US empire is The Devouring Mother with the big pharma interests representing the Munchausen by Proxy side of that archetype. That works as a po-litical explanation and this political dynamic exists for other western countries who are most directly in the orbit of the US empire. But, for Australia, it is also an excellent summation of our culture and in this we differ from other western nations in a way that explains why the archetype was able to manifest here so strongly. We used to refer to Britain as "the mother country". Australia was originally set up as a penal colony and populated with people who had been abandoned by their "mother". Kicked out of the house. Orphaned. The country was then utilised. We were initially a naval outpost of the British empire and are now a naval outpost of the US empire. Politically and culturally, we have never been fully independent and autonomous. By contrast, the US went to war with its mother and well and truly asserted its indepen-dence. Donald Horne said that Australia never "deserved" our institu-tions. They were part of our luck. We never earned them the hard way like America earned its independence. In relation to our shared "mother country", America is the rebellious child and Australia the acquiescent. We are also younger. The US declared independence two years before Australia was first settled by Britain. It took all the way until the 1970s for us to throw off the "cultural cringe" according to which we were necessarily inferior to the grand old cultures of Europe but that was just in time to fall under the influence of US culture and politics in the post war years.

If Australia has been politically The Orphan since its inception, it's also true that Australian culture displays the traits of The Orphan archetype. On the positive side, we like to get along with people. We are pragmatic and unpretentious to a fault. We are realist and conservative in our realism. Australians err on the side of caution in stark contrast to the US which errs on the side of big, idealist dreams. The shadow traits of The Orphan are also present here: cynicism, complaining, victimisation of others, powerlessness and worrying. Australians are notoriously cynical towards politicians. But this is merely an affectation. When the chips are down, as we have seen during corona, we turn to politicians to save us. The Nanny State has been dominant here for a long time. The desire to be saved and cared for is also a trait of The Orphan. The victimisation of others can be seen in what is known as Tall Poppy Syndrome where people who set out to achieve something out of the ordinary are cut down to size. Our anti-intellectualism and anti-elitism are other examples. This is in stark contrast to the US where the achiever, the entrepreneur and the iconoclast are celebrated. Powerlessness and worrying have been at the core of our corona response. A common response to anybody who questions that response is "what would you do?" or "there's no other option". We have been unable to raise a single dissenting voice because no sooner does somebody speak up than they are cut down to size. Having silenced those who would speak out, we say there is no alternative. This pattern was already present in Australian history. We used to accuse people of being "Un-Australian" if ever they said something critical of the country. If you spoke in disparaging terms of the nation, you were invited to "leave if you didn't like it". Earlier in our history, these traits led to a stifling atmosphere of conformism which many of our most talented artists and thinkers escaped by going – guess where? – back to the mother country in Britain. We thought we had thrown off that conformism, docility and servility in the 1970s but clearly we have not. There were always alternatives to lockdowns such as shown by Sweden and Florida (and later Alberta) but we convinced ourselves that the path we were on was the only one even as it was increasingly becoming clear that the path we were on was a road to nowhere. I mentioned above that Australian culture "hides away". This is much like The Orphan. We just want to fit in. We prefer to be liked than respected. We don't want to stick out. And ultimately, as corona has shown, we just want to be "safe".

The notion of safety has been at the centre of Australian political and cultural debate for almost the entirety of the nation's short history. To be fair, there were genuine issues at play. The population of the country was so small relative to the land mass as to be a weakness militarily. There were also economic issues. Much like immigration in the modern US is favoured by agricultural business interests, it was those interests which sought cheap labour primarily from the pacific islander nations during Australia's history (it's noteworthy that right in the middle of corona, Australia made special exemption for islanders to enter the country as they still form the backbone of the fruit and vegetable workers in this country). At the end of WW1, the Prime Minister, Billy Hughes, returned home from the armistice meetings and declared that Australia was now "safe" (from German and Japanese imperial ambitions). Another thing that Hughes brought home from Versailles was the continuation of the White Australia Policy. He thereby kept "safe" one of the cornerstones of Australian political debate at that time. The "White Australia Policy", in some form of another, stayed in place all the way into the 1970s and was still being actively defended by politicians as late as the 1960s. That policy is summed up very nicely in its own language – "This country shall remain forever the home of the descendants of those people who came here in peace in order to establish in the South Seas an outpost of the British race." An outpost of the British race? This is a reminder that the language and beliefs around "race" were not limited to the Germans in the pre-WW2 period. It also makes explicit how the Australians of that time saw themselves: just a part of the British empire. The White Australia policy aimed, among other things, to preserve racially purity by excluding other races, most notably the Chinese who arrived in large numbers during the gold rushes. Again, we should bear in mind that "race" and "civilisation" were at that time seen to be two sides of the same coin. In any case, the idea of Australia as an outpost of British civilisation held sway until WW2 when it was clear that the British empire could no longer provide security for the country. That security would in turn be provided by the Americans and Australia would shift from an outpost of Britain to a card-carrying member of the emerging globalist, multi-cultural paradigm of the US empire.

Against this historical backdrop, it is at first glance surprising that Australia should have transformed so quickly into one of the more successful multi-cultural nations in the world but that is what has happened in the last several decades. Interestingly, The Orphan archetype predicts this. Orphans get along with people. They are unpretentious and pragmatic. These are useful traits supporting a policy of multi-culturalism. Within this broad historical arc, one can see why Australian culture would be so hard to find. We went from the cultural cringe of subservience to the British to the multi-culturalism and globalism of the American empire very quickly. We have faithfully served the interests of both empires and have been among the most enthusiastic proponents of the neoliberal agenda in recent decades. Robin Boyd noted in the 1960s that this tendency to imitate first the British and then the Americans implied a culture that was not certain in itself. For Boyd, whose preoccupation was architecture, this amounted to an unwillingness to deal with the problem of "place". The Australian veneer was a mask that hid a deeper uncertainty. In archetypal terms, we still do not feel at home even in our own country and in our own skin. This is the uncertainty of The Orphan who has not established its place in the world.

Australian culture is talked about so seldom that it's hard to get a grasp on what foreigners think of us. Americans think of Australians via the stereotypes of the movies and television. We are Crocodile Dundee and Steve Irwin wrestling crocodiles and drinking beer in the sun. When George W Bush visited Australia during his presidency he said Australians were like Texans. That may be true of rural Australia, but most Australians do not live in the country or have anything much to do with it outside the occasional day trip. On the whole, Australians are far more like Californians. No surprise that the state in the US that most closely resembles our corona response was California. We are one of the most urbanised countries in the world and our big cities are really big, even by US standards. Unlike the US, we lack the large number of inland cities and our rural population is so sparse that it is politically almost irrelevant. Thus, modern Australia is the big, international city where you can eat food from all corners of the world and see people from all nations. It is the cosmopolitanism of Los Angeles or San Francisco but without the squalor and homelessness.

It was in a conversation with three foreigners who were living here that I got one of the more honest bits of feedback on Australian culture that I have heard and one that reveals The Orphan in our culture. In the group was an Indian, a Malaysian and a Singaporean. All three were professionals who had moved to Melbourne for work. The subject of Australian workplace culture came up and one of the three, who had clearly been mulling over the subject for some time, said "Australians are two faced". This got me intrigued. I had never heard that said about Australians before. In fact, I had barely heard anything negative said about Australians before. I asked her for clarification. The root of the problem was a part of Australian culture that I was very familiar with – our extreme aversion to conflict of any kind. Australians will do anything to avoid an argument. In this we show our British roots, only Australians tend to hide the matter behind an American-style forced positivity rather than the sophistication of subtle British mannerisms where avoiding conflict is a delicate dance. This is the flip side of The Orphan's inter-dependency strength. Orphans are good at getting along with others. But that strength can become an imperative for consensus and an unwillingness to hear dissenting opinions. Everybody must get along, or else. Australia has seen that in stark terms during corona with an almost complete inability to raise a dissenting voice in our public discourse. In the workplace, this manifests as an unwillingness to talk frankly with colleagues. It was this which had annoyed the Malaysian woman I was talking to. According to her, in Singapore and Malaysia it was normal to be told to your face by a colleague or superior if they thought you were doing something wrong. It was considered the right thing to do. In Australia, nobody does that. Rather, people will complain (another trait of The Orphan) to a superior and then it's the superior's job to handle it. That's what this woman meant when she said Australians were two-faced. They say one thing to your face and another thing behind your back. She was right to be upset because this is actually a form of predatory behaviour cloaked in niceness. This predatory behaviour manifests in other ways too such as the tall poppy syndrome. Avoiding disagreement is such an intrinsic part of the culture here that I was once made to take part in a workplace seminar on the subject of giving "negative feedback" (aka telling the truth to somebody about themselves and their performance). The strategy recommended was the "shit sandwich". You start by telling the person something that you like about their work. Then you slip in the negative feedback that's the thing that you really want to say and you finish with something positive. All that time and energy just to try and avoid speaking a basic truth that in other cultures would be taken care of with a normal conversation. That's life in a culture dominated by The Orphan archetype. Note also that this unwillingness to engage in truthful criticism also implies The Devouring Mother. The Devouring Mother will not speak the truth to her children, only false niceties. Australians watch the brutal discourse in US politics with mild horror. Arguably the US goes too far in the direction of heated argument. We go too far in the other. There is no debate, no meaningful disagreement in Australia and not because there are no issues but because we do not know how to disagree.

Of course, it's not the traits of The Orphan that made the Australian corona response international news but rather those of The Devouring Mother. What is perhaps most interesting about that is that it is genuinely out of character at the political level. In the normal course of events, Australian politics is excruciatingly boring. Superstar politicians like Trump or Obama would be a complete impossibility here. This is true at the federal level but it is even more pronounced at the state level. Prior to 2020, the average Australian would barely have been able to remember the name of the premier in the state where they lived and most would have failed to name those in any other states. But with corona it was the state premiers who suddenly held all the power as it is the states who are responsible for public health. Thus, once insignificant political figures were catapulted into prominence. What did they do with their new powers? They behaved exactly like Devouring Mothers with gaslighting, guilt tripping and emotional manipulation on a daily basis. The Australian public, forever cynical of any politician, suddenly dropped all cynicism and lapped up the manipulation without a second thought. What had happened was that the "child" archetype that dominates our culture had slipped into its shadow and The Devouring Mother had taken the reins of power. This makes sense when we consider that The Devouring Mother archetype requires a child. Australia as Orphan was already there and with corona we just needed The Devouring Mother to fill the gaps. Our politicians at the state level took up the role with aplomb.

Being a young country and only recently separated from the "mother country", Australian culture is the culture of the child in archetypal terms. Our requirement for safety is not, of itself, a bad thing. It is obviously a basic necessity. Where it turns negative is when it is clearly doing harm. This harm is at the core of The Devouring Mother – Child relationship and the harm being done is the stunted development of the child. To address this requires strength of character and the ability to speak truth. It's the desire to stand up and assert oneself. The absence of these is obliviousness and denial; the refusal to face hard truths. That is precisely where Australia found itself during corona; endless cycles of lockdown and the escalation of failed policies with no ability to face the facts. At time of writing, we have no meaningful plan to extricate ourselves from the current situation and I expect the plan that we do have to fall apart by the end of the year. It could very well be that Australia's borders remain closed for many years. History has a sense of irony. The country has returned to its roots. The isolationism, conformism and parochialism are back. Maybe in some sense they never really went away. They were just hidden beneath the veneer of neoliberal globalism. We were one of the most enthusiastic supporters of that doctrine. We watched on as Brexit and Trump happened and shook our heads. But these were the harbingers of what we now see and those chickens have now come home to roost here as elsewhere. We've all heard about the border wall between the US and Mexico. But border walls are going up in Europe now too. Neoliberal globalism seems to be evaporating right before our very eyes. Where does that leave Australia? I'm not sure we know and certainly nobody is talking about it. As yet, we have no rebellious children in this country; no Brexit and no Trump to chart any kind of alternative course into the future. The freedoms we thought we had were the freedoms that American citizens have and that are transmitted to us through US culture. But, as Robin Boyd noted, we have done nothing to earn them. And maybe we don't really believe in them. What we believe in is "safety" at all costs just like we have for all of our short history. Dissenting voices are not allowed at the best of times in Australia and with corona they have been completely smothered. For that reason, I expect Australia will have to wait for other countries to show us the way forward. Just as we have had to wait for other countries to deliver us the vaccine which is the non-solution to our situation. And, finally, we will have to wait, probably decades or more, before Australian culture in whatever form it eventually takes can break free of the dependency we have on "international western culture". Only once the US empire, our Devouring Mother, has retreated and we stand exposed to the world on equal terms will such a culture have a chance to develop. I used to think that time was far off in the future but it may be much closer that we think.

Politically speaking, The Devouring Mother *is* the US empire in its declining phase. The fact that the virus originated in China, the emerging competitor to that empire, is yet another synchronicity in the story.

The satellite states, the *acquiescent children* of the US empire – Australia, New Zealand and Canada – have been most affected. Meanwhile, the battle in the US was already against the rebellious children from within the empire itself who could fight back. This provides some explanation of the relative differences in the manifestation of the archetype within the Anglosphere in particular and western culture in general. It's also the case that western culture in general is prone to psychic epidemics due to a number of factors that Jung himself outlined explicitly and Australia suffers from these more than other western nations. Is it a coincidence that Americans as a nation are far more religious than other western nations, especially Australia? Jung saw the purpose of religion in adults, and myths and fairy tales in children, to allow the contents of the unconscious mind to be interpreted and integrated. If this does not happen, the energy from those unconscious contents works through the conscious mind leading to phobias, hypochondrias and psychic epidemics. Because the mythico-religious language to express such things is not available to an irreligious culture, these energies instead find expression in "rational" and "scientific" terms. When people say corona is a cult or a religion, they are sort of correct. In Jungian terms, it's the lack of religion which is the cause. The effect is the psychic epidemic. Australia has become an extremely irreligious nation in the post war years and this may also explain our blindness to the unconscious processes that have been at work during corona.

Appendix B: A Theoretical Discussion on Archetypes

Two of the common criticisms of Jungian archetypes are that they lack analytical rigor and that they are not causative, or at least can't be shown to be causative in the way we normally associate with science. It is no small irony, of course, that the field of virology suffers from similar difficulties. As I noted in The Plague Story, there are still no definitive rules by which to show that a virus causes an illness and this is especially true of respiratory viruses. Furthermore, the criteria about what constitutes a distinct virus that is different from other viruses have been changed a number of times recently and there is still much disagreement within virology about what they should be. Nevertheless, our society has had no problem believing that sars-cov-2 is a *new* virus and that it causes a *new* disease which is all the more surprising as this *new* disease seems to have no unique symptoms. It's mostly the same people who believe in that *science* who would criticise Jungian psychology for being unscientific.

There are strong parallels between Jungian psychology and the branch of knowledge I did my university degree in – linguistics. One of the things that is interesting about that is that modern linguistics aims for exactly the kind of rigor some would say is lacking in Jungian psychology. However, the underlying assumptions in linguistics are incredibly similar to those of Jung. Thus, we can use these as an analogy to try and shed light on the theoretical basis of Jungian analysis. Some people deny that the archetypes exist, but nobody would deny that the English language exists. Nevertheless, the two are comparable as *objects* of study and we should be able to use the latter to elucidate the former. In doing so, we'll also have a look at why the commonalities between linguistics and psychology makes them not amenable to the strict analytical rules and causal determination that can be achieved in the "hard" sciences. Before we get to that, though, let's do a lightning review of the main moves in 20th century linguistics wrought by the man whose work overturned the discipline, Noam Chomsky.

One of the main tasks Chomsky set for linguistics was how to account for the ages-old problem of how children learn language. We know that every child with faculties intact will learn language to native speaker level automatically and without conscious effort as long as they are exposed to spoken language during what is known as the critical period (roughly the time from birth until puberty). We also know that a child will learn the language of wherever they happen to be in the world even though the languages of the world show radical diversity in form. And we know that whatever language the child is exposed to, the actual raw data they get, the spoken language, is imperfect and incomplete. As I write this book, I am correcting myself as I go and I have the ability to go over what I have written and correct errors afterwards. But we can't do that with spoken language. A transcript of me reading this exact same text out loud, even if I was reading directly from the written material, would show errors, false starts and other inconsistencies. Every-day, spontaneous spoken language contains even more errors, false starts and incomplete sentences and that is before you factor in metaphorical language or creative and novel use of forms and all the other bits and pieces that add spice to the spoken word. The task for the language learning child of bringing order to his mess seems insurmountable if the child was using general deduction to try and ascertain the rules of the language. Therefore, Chomsky posited that there must exist a faculty of some kind which is innate and whose structure the child brings to the problem so that it *knows* most of the rules in advance at some level of abstraction. Its job in language learning is to figure out how the language it is hearing fits onto those pre-existing rules. Because these rules are limited, the child would have a relatively small set of options to choose from and the task of language learning becomes manageable. Chomsky called this innate faculty Universal Grammar and we can map what this looks like as follows:-

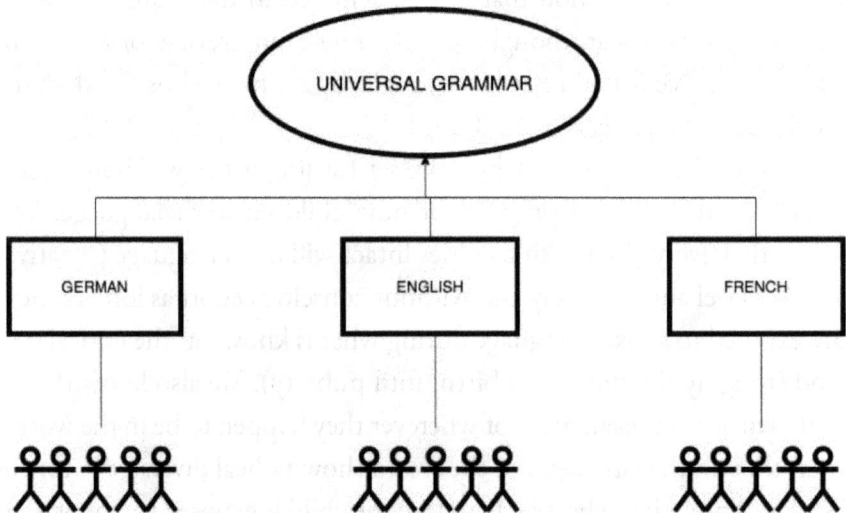

This diagram refers to individual speakers, a specific language spoken by a community of those speakers and the Universal Grammar whose rules govern the possible forms of individual languages. Of course, Universal grammar must be *in* each of us in a form that it can be handed down through the generations. Meanwhile, what we call a language is itself an abstraction from the everyday spoken word. The linguist deduces a grammar from the linguistic behaviour of a community of speakers. This language is always in flux and its vocabulary, syntax and phonetic patterns change over time. Nevertheless, within the Chomskyan paradigm, it is hypothesised that the grammar will always map back to the abstract rules of Universal Grammar which every one of us has in our mental makeup. By analysing the rules of each language spoken in the world, we should be able to hypothesise and then prove the rules of Universal Grammar. In doing so, we would account for how children acquire language and we would shine a scientific light into the previously dark recesses of human cognition. That was, in a nutshell, the goal which Chomsky set and which made linguistics, at least for a few decades, one of the most exciting fields of study in the 20th century.

There are problems with the Chomskyan program which we don't need to go into here. However, this way of formulating the question of the way we learn language is almost beyond doubt. Linguists will argue about the nature of the faculties used in language acquisition but nobody doubts that there must be some innate faculties the child brings to the job. What Chomsky was trying to do was to bring the issue down to concrete, testable hypotheses and thereby to arrive over time at a more precise understanding of the language faculty. What is of relevance to us is that this way of framing things is identical to what Jung had in mind with his archetypes. In fact, the exact same diagram can be drawn to characterise Jung's theory of the archetypes:

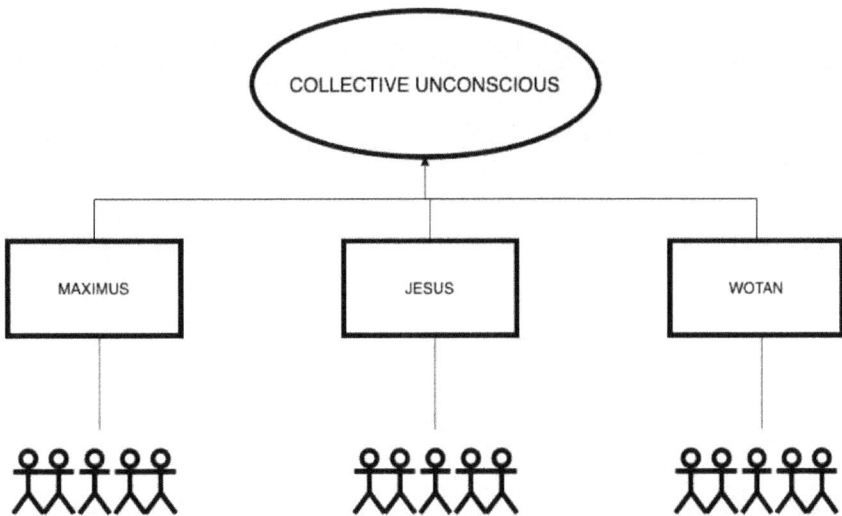

What Maximus (the character in the movie Gladiator), Jesus and Wotan are meant to represent here are culturally specific examples of archetypes which bear the same relation to the collective unconscious as a specific language such as English bears to Universal Grammar. Jung would posit that there exists a more abstract form of each archetype in the Collective Unconscious which governs the expression in a particular culture. Thus, Maximus is one possible manifestation of The Warrior archetype in the same way that English is one possible manifestation of a human language. Just like Chomsky and other linguists study the patterns of language to try and determine the more abstract forms of Universal Grammar, so Jung studied the psychological manifestations of the archetypes to try and arrive back at the more abstract forms. At this resolution, the two methods seem the same. However, Chomsky created a detailed and highly technical analysis of syntactic forms in his generative grammar whereas Jung did not aim for anything like that level of precision. In my opinion, what happened with Chomskyan linguistics is that the generative grammar became a complex game in its own right and this became a distraction from the underlying goal. What's more, it doesn't appear to have worked. The early results, which seemed promising, were limited by a focus on syntax and specifically the syntax of English. As the model was applied to other languages the limitations of this approach became clear. There are languages in the world where syntax simply isn't that relevant and where morphology does most of the heavy lifting. In such languages, generative grammar becomes a clumsy and laborious way to account for the language and this throws doubt on the relation back to Universal Grammar. It looks to me like Chomsky's project fell into the kind of category error that we'll have a look at shortly and the purported rigor and detailed technical analysis actually left out a great deal that was essential to language itself. That's the problem with the reductionist approach: how do you know that the things you are excluding from consideration aren't important? Meanwhile, the criticisms of Jung become less credible. Jung specifically said the archetypes were general and inherently subjective. There was no point in aiming for a precision which couldn't be achieved and the more general approach has the virtue of flexibility, something which was lacking in Chomsky.

It's instructive that one of the criticisms labelled against Chomsky was that, for all his purported scientific rigor, ultimately he had to rely on the intuitions of individual speakers of a language to decide what was and was not grammatical. His *rules* were based on such intuitions but, within the edicts of materialist science, that is bad form. We need empirically verifiable data and not subjective data. As we just noted, this same accusation has been levelled against Jung and he was fully aware of the criticism and the underlying philosophical position which motivates it. In order to see why it is invalid, let's have a look at a way of dividing up the domains of knowledge that I first read about in Gregory Bateson's book *Mind and Nature*. We'll see that both linguistics and psychology are related disciplines that fall into a separate category from the hard sciences. Because of that, they can and do share an approach to knowledge that is valid within that domain but would be considered invalid in the domain of hard science.

The domains that Bateson outlined are *pleroma* and *creatura*. To pleroma belongs the two disciplines that we generally consider to be hard science: physics and chemistry. To creatura belongs disciplines such as linguistics and psychology as well as biology, medicine, hermeneutics and religious and spiritual pursuits. The following diagram gives an outline of this distinction.

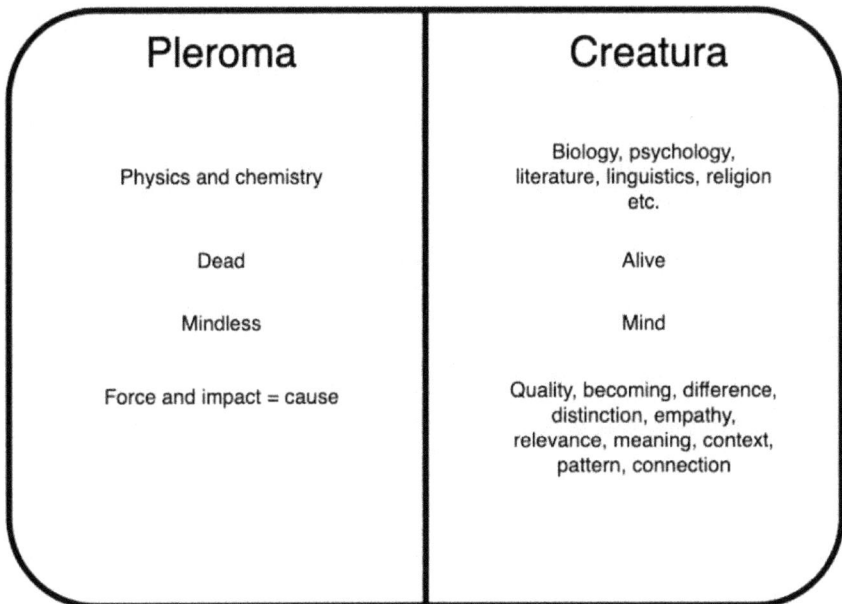

Pleroma	Creatura
Physics and chemistry	Biology, psychology, literature, linguistics, religion etc.
Dead	Alive
Mindless	Mind
Force and impact = cause	Quality, becoming, difference, distinction, empathy, relevance, meaning, context, pattern, connection

We can see that a category error occurs whenever we apply the methods which are valid in pleroma to creatura and vice versa. The latter of these is what is usually called superstition while the former is sometimes called scientism. What Chomsky was trying to do in linguistics is also what many others have been trying to do in the 20th and into the 21st centuries which is to apply the methods of science from the pleroma domain to the creatura domain. Chomsky's appeal to intuition, however, was more in keeping with the domain of creatura and was for this reason criticised by those who think that only pleroma methods can yield truth. But this is exactly what Bateson, Jung and others would have denied. There were various movements and schools of thought in the 20th century that set out to put the domain of creatura on a firm footing and try to address the imbalance that had arisen where the methods valid to pleroma had come to be seen as the be all and end all of knowledge; what was sometimes called *physics envy*. The creatura domain is always in the process of becoming. It simply can't yield the static, reproducible results that we find in the *dead* world of pleroma. Moreover, in Bateson's analysis, all the creatura domain is governed by *mind* and because mind implies a hierarchy of logical types and feedback loops up and down the hierarchy, it's not possible to do reductionist science because the attempt at reductionism at best sets a new context which didn't exist before and at worst outright changes the very object under study. Bateson would also have said that empathy is needed in the domain of creatura. It takes a mind to know a mind. That's why linguistics must appeal to the intuitive judgements of speakers about what is and is not grammatical. Only a speaker of a language can know those things. If you try and remove the speaker from the equation, you lose something fundamental. This is exactly what happens in certain types of cognitive science research where the researcher will often hide the true intent of the study from the subject. They give the subject a task to do while the thing that the researcher is trying to test for is orthogonal to that task. In that way, the subject's rational mind will not "get in the way" of the results. In doing so, the researcher has removed conscious awareness from the equation. Such results may have a certain validity but I think we can all agree that conscious awareness is a pretty important thing to be leaving out when it comes to human beings. That's what happens when you apply the pleroma paradigm to the creatura domain. Even within Chomskyan linguistics, with its pretension to *hard science*, that I am a native speaker of English gives me the right to make judgements about the whole of the English language. Bateson said the same in relation to biology. As biological creatures, we can compare ourselves to other biological creatures and determine the patterns which connect us. The same goes for Jungian psychology. Each of us is a psyche and, if we can recognise the elements of the psyche within us, we can also recognise it without. *Know thyself* then becomes a practical requirement in the pursuit of truth in the domain of creatura.

The *messiness* of human language mirrors the *messiness* of human psychology. But the desire to clean up this messiness is not valid in the domain of creatura. Even in the hard sciences, the preference for simplicity known as Occam's Razor is mostly a practical matter. For any simple explanation there are numerous, perhaps infinite, explanations that *work* to account for a phenomenon. We just prefer the simplest one. However, to paraphrase Einstein, explanations should be as simple as possible but no simpler. By leaving out so much of what makes language what it is, Chomsky might have won some insights into syntax but he left out a whole lot of other things that are arguably just as important. As Mary Midgely noted, this zeal for reductionism, which she called reductionist megalomania, when applied to the domain of creatura leads to results that miss the point by excluding from consideration that which cannot be excluded.

Jung did not deny the validity of the hard sciences. Rather, he argued that the part of our mind that can think causally and rationally is actually quite young and is built upon a much larger and much more well-established part of the mind that interprets the world acausally or, we might say, religiously or symbolically. Many of the greatest scientists believed much the same thing and did not deny the validity of the older way of understanding. It is only in the modern world with our extremist materialist philosophy that the denial of that way of thinking has become common. We demand causal explanations based on quantity and number but when these are applied to the domain of creatura we leave out that which is crucial to our understanding. Consider this, virology actually sits right on the border between pleroma and creatura. We call it a part of biology but it deals with viruses and viruses are not alive. If we were to say that virology was actually a part of organic chemistry we would be placing it inside the pleroma domain. That would make clear a distinction which has not been clear during corona which is that virology and viral disease are two very different things. The former has as its object a virus while the latter has as its object the *relation* between a virus and a person (medicine) and the *relation* between a virus and a population (epidemiology). These latter two disciplines of study are in the domain of creatura and this would make clear the fact that we would not want to apply the methods that are valid in pleroma to those disciplines. But, in fact, the whole corona discourse has been based on exactly that. The obsessive counting of "cases" is just one aspect of that category error. The same people who are happy to gloss over the analytical difficulties of viral disease are the ones who would deny archetypal analysis because it does not establish causality. That correlation does not imply causality is one of the basic principles of hard science and yet it is correlation that has driven the whole corona business.

Psychologically speaking, the corona event has been driven by those older faculties of the mind that Jung described and not the younger, scientific faculties and yet it's the people who deride those older faculties as superstition who have been most susceptible to them. In a way, that's not surprising. If you aren't used to using those faculties, you are going to be defenceless in the same way that somebody who has no fighting skills is defenceless against a trained martial artist. Our modern materialist society pretends those faculties don't exist and so we have a population of people who are completely blind to what is still the main driver of human affairs. We pretend that the rationalist tip of the iceberg is all that exists while being wilfully ignorant of the power and mass of the submerged subconscious. Thus, the error in corona has been the same error that Bateson and the other systems thinkers and cyberneticists had already identified in the 20th century: a category error of believing that only the precepts of reductionist science can give rise to knowledge and the invalid application of those precepts to the creatura domain. What is required in the creatura domain is the acceptance of holistic thinking. It's a generalist approach that uses what the philosopher Charles Sanders Peirce called *abductive reasoning*. This involves drawing inferences across domains or looking for what Bateson called the pattern which connects. What abductive reasoning implies, and it is this which most offends against our materialist prejudices, is that certainty is not attainable. This is exactly what Jung claimed in relation to what we can know about the archetypes. Such an approach requires the opposite of reductionist megalomania and an acceptance of epistemic humility. By failing to acknowledge this, we do what we have done during corona which amounts to nothing more than a desperate grasping after a certainty which can never be attained. We attempt to simplify things which cannot and should not be simplified and in so doing we fall into the trap outlined by the old saying – we cut off our nose to spite our face.

REFERENCES

Chapter 1

1. https://www.youtube.com/watch?v=UIDsKdeFOmQ&t=4s
2. https://www.researchgate.net/publication/341832637_All-cause_mortality_dur-ing_COVID-19_No_plague_and_a_likely_signature_of_mass_homicide_
3. https://swprs.org/facts-about-covid-19/
4. https://theconversation.com/routine-mammograms-do-not-save-lives-the-research-is-clear-84110

Chapter 3

1. https://www.msn.com/en-gb/health/familyhealth/jordan-peter-son-said-he-s-getting-a-covid-vaccine-and-anti-vax-fans-are-furi-ous/ar-BB1gIMGQ

NOTE TO THE READER

Please consider leaving a review of this book on your favourite review site. All reviews, positive and negative, are a great help.

More information on Simon Sheridan, including a semi-regular blog, can be found at https://simonsheridan.me

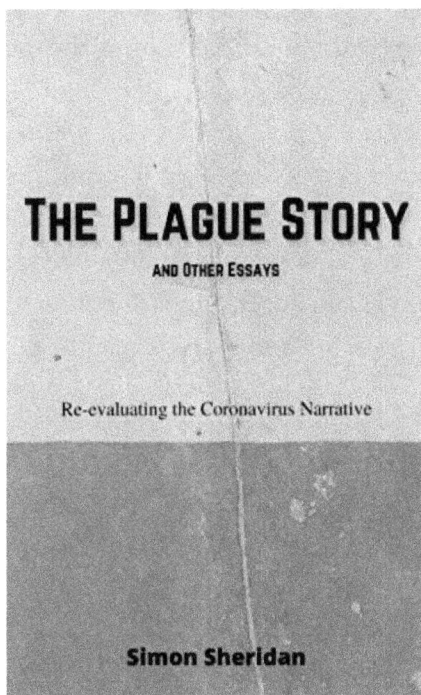

THE PLAGUE STORY
AND OTHER ESSAYS

Re-evaluating the Coronavirus Narrative

Simon Sheridan

"Those who tell the stories rule society" - Plato

Societies run on stories. But in the modern west, we believe that we are above stories; we are scientific. It is partly because of this (story!) that we are often blind to the stories we tell ourselves. In this book, I analyse the structure of the story we have been telling ourselves about the corona event: the plague story. I look at how the plague story unfolded and who has been telling it. The structure of that story dictates both what has happened so far and what needs to happen to bring the matter to an end.

There's just one problem: corona is clearly not a plague. Therefore, our willingness to accept it as such needs explanation. In the second half of the book, I sketch out the larger social and cultural themes that have been at work. Among these are our growing biophobia and denial of death, our continuing belief in the myths of heroic science and progress, the tension between technocracy and democracy, the economic and cultural realities wrought by globalisation and how the corona event fits within the founding and dominant ethos of the modern west: heroic materialism.

The Plague Story is a work that draws inspiration from the systems thinking and cybernetics movements of the 20th century. It is a multi-disciplinary series of essays that aims to place the corona event in the broader cultural and philosophical context of modern society. If you have the feeling that the story of corona is not quite right, this book aims to provide a framework for understanding and a guide to meaningful re-evaluation.